Ministries:
Sharing God's Gifts

Ministries: Sharing God's Gifts

by
James B. Dunning

A PACE Book
SAINT MARY'S PRESS
Christian Brothers Publications
Winona, Minnesota

Cover design by Henry Gerth

ISBN: 0-88489-123-2
Library of Congress Catalog Card Number: 80-52058

Contents

Introduction

This book was written during the months of transition between the seventies and the eighties.

Caricatures of past decades have been abundant. We have had slogans about the myopic fifties, the militant sixties, the mystic seventies.

No logic dictates that the turn of a decade need produce a new personality for the eighties. Yet, in the secular world, *Newsweek* magazine, in the summer of '79, quotes commentators on the contemporary scene who claim that the inactivity and negativism of the seventies may bring us to the brink of a new age of creativity in the eighties. The present fragmentation of the American people concerning goals and values clamors, it is said, for common purpose and direction in the next decade. Our energies, which have become limited at the gas stations and oil refineries, must expand when it comes to global consciousness and commitment to common values. Moreover, all this calls for a leadership spread among more people and not concentrated on charismatic leaders who could not possibly pull off this grand design today.

In the religious world, Church historian Martin Marty also talks of the end of a mini-era. He claims that the seventies ended for the Church with the Jonestown suicide event and that the introspection which led to bizarre cults in religion is declining. This change may also signal a turn from sometimes prophetic and sometimes demonic charismatic leadership to a rediscovery of gifts closer to home, spread out among the Christian community, experienced in small gatherings of Christians in our neighborhoods, our parishes, and in such movements as Marriage Encounter and Cursillo.

For many people, *ministry* has become the word which expresses their part in this diffusion of leadership and of gifts. For some Roman Catholics, "ministry" is still a reference to Protestant ministers, and for others sounds too official and clerical. For many others, however, the term seems to affirm the value of what they do inside and outside of church sanctuaries to hear and to express the presence of God and his Christ in the world. For the purpose of this book, the term is not important. What is important is the diffusion of leadership and the diffusion of gifts.

In Christian faith, such expansion of ministries will find its roots in our images of God, Christ, and Church. This little book, therefore, is basically an exercise in imagination. Chapter 1 offers a few images of that humanity created by God in his image. Chapter 2 offers an image of God present in the world, in his people, and most powerfully in Jesus Christ. Chapter 3 reflects on our image of Jesus who *is* God's presence in the world, and who communicates that presence in his humanity through ministries of Word, community-building, celebrating, and serving-healing. The next four chapters speak of us, the people of God whose humanity is charged with the Spirit of the Risen Christ, who image his presence in some of those same ways because we believe his presence is spread out among all his people. The final chapter gathers the strands together for some concluding reflections on ministries.

Two personal notes. First, my own theological roots would be with those moved by the insights of Karl Rahner. Some claim that, although Rahner is sensitive to evil, to sin, and to the immense fragility of humankind, his final word is always one of redemption, resurrection, goodness, and hope. This book springs from that same hope. The image of the human grounded in our tradition of the "imago Dei" speaks more of our possibilities than our stumblings and bumblings. Some may find this naive, perhaps even the approach of a Pollyanna. I hope not. G. K. Chesterton once claimed that hope is a virtue only when things look hopeless. Otherwise, it's just logic. My sense is that, in those terms, these are times for hope. We have gone through the turmoils of the sixties with the American tragedies of Vietnam and Watergate which led into the seeming stagnation of the seventies. We have heard about our sins and failures. It seems to me that, just as there were prophets of judgment in Israel when she was blind to her sins and prophets of hope when she fell to her knees, our coming decade calls for some words of hope about our grand possibilities if we arouse our faith in God and his images.

Second, I write as a priest (a cohort of those who have monopolized official ministries for a few centuries) and also as one whose principal ministry has been the continuing education of priests. I am convinced that priests will be spiritual leaders precisely by helping people discern: how God has spread out his gifts, how they might share those gifts in ministries, and how we all might celebrate and thank God for those gifts. In those terms, the lives of priests will be fulfilled when those gifts are discerned, shared, and celebrated. I am also convinced that the most helpful continuing education of priests takes place in dialogue with other ministers in contexts where we can share our experiences and clarify how all of us might best share the unique gifts which are ours. I hope that this book will make a modest contribution to that dialogue.

The Process

To assist that dialogue, both within yourself and with others, each chapter offers two reflection aids.

The "Where I Stand" section allows you to write each chapter before you read it and to rewrite both your own reflections and mine after reading it. I hope this process will give you a chance to talk with me and also with yourself, so that these reflections on ministries help you discern "where *you* stand" regarding God, Christ, Church, your own gifts, and your own ministry.

You may want to share the above as well as the "Conversation Starters" with other people. The conversation starters are not aimed at conceptual understanding so much as at clarifying your own experiences and values regarding ministries. One caution: in group sharing, no one should be forced to share what he/she does not want to share. Some of the questions might raise issues which tap strong feelings and convictions. The explicit contract of your group should be to respect others' privacy and freedom to respond at the level they choose.

One further note: I have taken a random approach with the conversation starters. Feel free to choose those questions which would most likely launch the conversations you want to start.

Acknowledgments

I would like to thank all those who ministered to me in the preparation of this book: Mary Perkins Ryan who has given so much to help a Church of many ministries be reborn, and who has edited this volume with insight, patience, and care; graduate students in my class at St. Michael's College in Winooski, Vermont, who proofread the text and bounced these reflections off their own experience; Christiane Brusselmans and George Weigel who helped clarify these ideas through our workshops together; my confreres of the National Organization for Continuing Education of Roman Catholic Clergy (NOCERCC) who opened so many new avenues of approach to ministries; and most especially Archbishop Hunthausen and the Church of Seattle where, with some fits and starts, these ministries are taking flesh in exciting ways. It is from this Church, and especially from family and friends within this Church, that I have learned all that I know and cherish about Christian ministries.

1 More Than We Could Imagine

Where I Stand

Directions: Complete the following sentences before and after reading the following chapter. Doing so *before* reading will help you write the chapter from your own experience. Doing so *after* reading may lead you to amend parts of the chapter or to change your own thoughts and feelings. This process will help you clarify where you stand and what you want to share with others.

1) When people talk of God's presence in me, I feel . . .

2) When people talk of God's presence in others, I feel . . .

3) My three greatest gifts are . . .

4) My three greatest weaknesses are . . .

5) During the past five years I have grown more confident about . . .

6) I am happiest when . . .

7) I am most discouraged when . . .

8) About the human image of God, I believe . . .

9) About the value of psychology for understanding my faith, I believe . . .

Let the first words about ministry be words about God. Let the Good News be that ministry is not our task, our creation, or even our burden. The Good News is that ministry is God's creation because *we* are

God's creation. Ministry is "more than we could imagine" because it is God who did the "imagining." "Let us make man in our image, after our likeness . . . so God created man in his own image, in the image of God he created him" (Gen. 2:7, 1:26-27). *God is present in his image, and ministry is revealing and sharing the gift of his presence.*

A few years ago I received the following letter from a young man who voices a faith that it is God who is the giver of gifts which we share with others:

Dear Jim:

When I was a child, my parents used to take us every year to the parish carnival. They would give us a buck to spend on anything we wanted. One time after we got back into our car to go home, they asked me if I had a good time. I sat in silence, then burst into tears, opened my hand and showed them my buck. You see, I was afraid to spend it, afraid to let go of it, because I thought I might make a mistake, get something I didn't want, and never get a buck again.

Well, what happened to me last year, poetically, was that people helped me spend my buck. And it was great, letting go, getting confidence that I had something to spend. And you know what? After I spent that first buck, I looked in my pocket and found another and another and another. And God is good, so are his people, and so, baby, am I!

Love,
Terry

Despite inflationary times, many people are discovering new ways to "spend their buck." Christians spend their buck in what they call ministries. I simply want to assert from the beginning that when motivated by Christian faith, ministers find their source of life in more than humanism, good will, philanthropy, and social activism. Certainly those latter qualities motivate many Christians. Indeed, they should since they proclaim that Christians have moved from an anti-human stance of earlier times. The 1960s especially began with a rollicking faith in the human. In a rebound, however, from those humanistic sixties, those turbulent days which began with the exuberance of New Frontiers and Wars on Poverty and ended with the collapsed frontiers of American fallibility in Vietnam and limits of energy and justice at home, I recently saw in the more realistic seventies a bumper sticker which proclaimed: "God is back—and He's mad!"

Terry proclaims that same message in more gentle tones. "God is good, so are his people, and so, baby, am I!" Genesis echoes in our times: God is good and we are "very good," created in his image, after his likeness. Nineteen centuries before us, St. Irenaeus also affirms that the good God makes the good man, and the good man finds the fullness of life in God:

> The glory of God
> is man fully alive
>
> and the full life of man
> is man seeing God.
>
> The showing forth of God
> which he made through creation
> gives life to everything that lives on earth:
>
> even more, that revealing of the Father
> which comes through the Word
> gives full life to men who see God.
>
> [*Adversus Haereses*, Bk. 4, 20:7]

Pardon the masculine language, by the way, in both Genesis and Irenaeus. The words have simply rung in our ears too long to say, "Let us make persons in our image," and "The glory of God is persons fully alive." More important is the faith behind the language—that our life and our ministries are not grounded in "masculine" control, power, "true grit," and self-made gifts but rather in "feminine" openness, receptivity, and sensitivity to the presence and initiative of God which should be true of both males and females. We are made by God, for God.

Because "masculine" qualities of power and control so often mark our Church, I made the first words in this book about ministries words about God and our "feminine" dependence on God. Because we Americans have our pioneer spirit and because ministries in that milieu can rise from an arrogant faith in our own power, our gifts, and our activism, I proclaimed the roots of ministry to be in God's presence in us whom he created in his image. Paradoxically, we shall see that the man who was *the* image of God and most fully God's man and God's minister was most dependent on his Father, empty of self, powerless, a man full of pain and suffering, struck down by human evil and sin, a man fully alive only through being a man fully dead. Therefore, let the first words of ministry be words about God.

Words about Us

Having given God the first word, we now give the second word to us. In a later chapter we need to ponder the controversy between those who limit the term "ministry" to persons who are officially ordained, installed, commissioned, or recognized by the Church as institution and those who assert that every Christian is called to ministry by baptism. Those who adopt the second, broader approach to ministry ground ministry on the Christian call to worship and service given at the time of baptism (more precisely, it should be initiation into the Church in baptism-confirmation-Eucharist). For example, the United States Bishops' Committee on Liturgy stated: "In the 1960s, we saw the development of *lay ministry* which is built on the premise that ministry is the privilege and responsibility of the total Church and everyone is called by baptism to exercise it, each in his own way and according to his own call and gifts."

Much talk about ministry has taken the first, institutional approach, and it has been very "churchy." It limits ministry to ordained clerics—bishops, priests, and deacons—or to installed or commissioned ministries such as Eucharistic ministers, lectors, acolytes, perhaps parish councils. This in its worst form means the ministry of "church mice" (I recently heard that the equivalent French idiom is "frogs in the holy water font"!) but in its best form identifies those persons who officially express for all of us, by their faith and compassion, the presence of God in his Church.

I noted that others who assert a universal call to all Christians to minister ground that call in baptism. I would like to extend the roots even deeper, back to God's creation of every woman and man in his image and likeness. There is an old scholastic axiom, *agere sequitur esse*, "our actions flow from our very being." In this case, our ministerial actions flow from our being as images of God, the place of his presence. When we discover his presence in us through faith in Christ and become baptized Christians, we all receive the Christian vocation to share that presence. But, in a sense, we can say there is an earlier calling to share what we are—images of God. Baptism does not make us images of God; baptism celebrates it. In baptism we accept the call; but the gentle voice of God has already whispered to us at creation and birth, "Become what you are." Even though we are touched by evil and by the sin of the human family, God is still present to everyone born in his image and likeness and calls them to reveal and share his presence.

It is appropriate, therefore, to continue our reflections on ministry with some words about us, based upon a look at the human stuff which God has made in his image. From our experience of the human, what is there about us that confirms the Good News of Genesis that we are images of the Lord?

In the next chapter we shall look at the persons in our Judaeo-Christian tradition whom God has confirmed to represent his image. Here we examine, however, the behavioral sciences—or, specifically, humanistic psychology. The father of this school, Abraham Maslow, claims that these psychologists differ from psychoanalysts and behaviorists in that they are concerned about human health and growth, not just with what makes people sick. The question, then, is this: Might studies of healthy humans, research on the qualities of humanity at its best, give some hints of what human beings have to offer each other in care and compassion? Might we also discover what kind of humanity we are called to build through that care and compassion? Christians find that humanity primarily in Jesus; but there is another Christian axiom, "holiness is wholeness." The holy person is one who is gifted by an integrated, healthy humanness. Although Jesus is our norm, can we discover, with the help of the humanistic psychologists, traits of that holy, healthy humanness to which we are called? Can what they have to say about us and our human vocation give some credence to our Christian vocation to be God's images?

In my doctoral dissertation I studied the theme of health and creativity in the works of certain humanistic psychologists. Although there were many individual differences, five common and fundamental characteristics of healthy, creative human beings emerged from this study. Although I find the psychologists I researched to be excessively ebullient about human possibility and naive about human perversity and sin, in the style of Jesus they do summon us to the best in ourselves through these calls to human health.

The Call to Communion with Self

Studies of healthy, creative persons reveal their tremendous abilities for communion with *all* dimensions of their humanity: their unconscious life, their memories and dreams, their bodies, their emotions and sensory experiences (some claim twenty-four senses have now been identified), their fantasies, their intuitions, and their various dimensions of intelligence. These people, when confronted with life's problems and possibilities, dip into the reservoir of their own humanity with ease. This is true not only of the artist whose humanity flows into his brush tip. It is true for the grandmother and grandfather whose humanity and richness of experience flow into care for their families.

The humanistic psychologists insist that all these dynamisms call us from within. They clamor for our attention and beg to be expressed in our lives. Maslow suggests, however, that only about five percent of us actually develop our own unique dynamisms of self. Why the miserable track record? The humanists blame the failure largely on environment, especially those demonic forces in our early years which destroy or erode self-esteem. Perhaps this says much about the ministry of parents and teachers who treat children with care and respect.

These psychologists also insist that when our basic physical and psychological needs are met—e.g., for food and self-esteem—then, from within our humanity, we hear the higher call for truth, beauty, justice, joy, wholeness, integrity. They claim the human organism calls for development from within by intrinsic growth tendencies which can be frustrated by environment but which continue to demand fulfillment even when denied. One dimension of the human vocation is to release the floodgates of the powers within us.

I ran across this description of potential energy, attributed to Thomas Wolfe, in a study of creativity done by a large corporation:

> It seemed that I had inside me, swelling and gathering all the time, a huge black cloud and that this cloud was loaded with electricity, pregnant, crested, with a kind of hurricane violence that could not be held in check much longer; that the moment was approaching fast when it must break. Well, all I can say is that the storm did break. It came in a torrent, and it is not over yet.

Someone once called Thomas Wolfe a "genius without talent," an ordinary man who heard the call from those energies within himself—energies which most of us ignore. What might happen if the rest of us "geniuses without talent" let these energies and gifts emerge and offered them in ministry?

The Call to Communion with the World

The creative person is also intensely conscious of persons, events, and things in the universe which call to her/him for communion. For psychologists, key words for the human vocation include: unity, integration, interaction, activity-between, at-oneness, synthesis, relationship. They call man/woman: a being-in-the-world, a spirit-in-the-world, a being-with-others who comes to personal fulfillment through relationship and inter-communion. In fact, the others do not remain others. The "out there" becomes the "in here." Inner and outer worlds merge with no rigid boundaries between the self and others. Our use of the beautiful word "intercourse"—literally, "between-running" or "flowing back and forth"—should not be limited just to sexual intercourse. It expresses what happens in all forms of communion between persons. The values, attitudes, and ways of the other become part of us, part of who we are, in such a way that we are enriched as the unique person we are.

The humanistic psychologists sound so optimistic and positive about our humanity, but they see our union with others also coming through pain and suffering. To feel the pain of another, to reach out with compassion (literally, to "suffer-with" in Latin), summons forth our energies through communion with the birth pains of the human family.

If ministry includes helping people experience communion with others and their world, think of all who ministered in this way: the poet, Gerard Manley Hopkins, in touch with what he called the "dearest freshness deep down things," who shared his communion with us; the artist, Pablo Picasso, who said, "I let nothing pass me by," and painted a world for us to enjoy. Think also of the man and woman in love who enable each other to experience most deeply the ways two humans can have intercourse with each other; the parents who explore with their children the wonders of the universe; all those who seek to heal the wounds of injustice and reconcile the fragmented members of humankind.

The Call to Search for Meaning

In a marvelous passage from *Cat's Cradle*, Kurt Vonnegut writes of the human vocation to question life and search for meaning:

> And God said, "Let us make living creatures out of mud, so the mud can see what We have done." And God created every living creature that now moveth—and one was man. Mud-as-man alone could speak. God leaned close as mud-as-man sat up, looked around and spoke. Man blinked, "What is the purpose of all this?" he asked politely. "Everything must have a purpose?" asked God. "Certainly," said man. "Then I leave it to you to think of one for all this," said God. And He went away.

Creative, healthy people do not simply receive stimuli from inside and outside themselves. They are driven from within by a passion to understand what the purpose is of all this. When life seems aimless, paltry, devoid of purpose, more full of the tragic than the gracious, then they sing with Peggy Lee, "Is that all there is?" "What's it all about, Alfie?"

Yet creative people are more stimulated than decimated by disorder and chaos. The tragedies of natural calamities, sickness and death, violence and oppression among humans—all stimulate their energies to bring order where there is disorder, healing where there are wounds, and even to discover some meaning where there is apparent meaninglessness. In regard to the latter, Viktor Frankl says that although human persons invented the gas chambers of Auschwitz, they also entered those chambers upright, with the Lord's Prayer or the Shema Israel on their lips. Even in the midst of the most terrible evil inflicted upon our brothers and sisters, some affirmed the meaning and value of dying with faith and dignity.

Think of the ministry of the incurably ill who find meaning in their sufferings and witness to us of courage and hope. Think of those who minister healing or at least mercy in our prisons, our hospitals, and homes for the aged and handicapped. Think of the so-called handicapped, the "little ones" in mind or body, who minister simple openness and acceptance to those of us handicapped by pride or selfishness. Think of citizens and public servants and community organizers who seek to discover and restore pattern and purpose in our urban neighborhoods and rural communities. Think of friends and relatives and counsellors who help middle aged persons adjust and redirect their energies after the normal failures of early life and discover new ideals and values. Think of those who cherish the experience and wisdom of people in their old age so that their last years have meaning and purpose. There are some great searchers for meaning who invite others into the human adventure and search.

The Call to Self-Actualization and Self-Transcendence

I combine these last two recurrent themes among the humanistic psychologists because they are intimately connected and sum up what has already been said.

Abraham Maslow, in particular, speaks of our vocation to communion with self and with others and our search for meaning in terms of the theme of self-actualization, i.e., the fulfillment of all the built-in dynamisms which are uniquely our own. He distinguishes between the special-talent creativity of the genius and the self-actualizing creativity which brings to fruition the unique potentialities of each individual. He asserts that every person is called from within and without to allow his/her own gifts to emerge.

But Viktor Frankl adds the theme of self-transcendence (reaching beyond self) as a healthy corrective to the goal of self-actualization. He claims the paradox is that if a person sets out to fulfill himself or herself, just as if he/she sets out to "get" friendship or happiness or love, he/she is doomed to frustration. Friendship, happiness, love, and self-actualization are gifts. They are discovered by receptivity to others, openness to life and events, reaching out with what philosopher Martin Heidegger calls "active waiting," not for the purpose of fulfilling ourselves but for the purpose of offering self in care and service. Then the mystery is that others in their freedom do respond; and in the giving away of our gifts we find they return to us multiplied a hundredfold. If self-transcendence marks our lives and our ministries, we create a ministry of service and not a ministry based on status or self-assertion through power over people. Jesus' words would mark our ministry: if we lose ourselves in care and self-giving we shall find ourselves.

This is the "faith" of the humanistic psychologists, in very brief compass. The Judaeo-Christian faith affirms, as the great German theologian Karl Rahner put it, that "the revelation of God to man *is* man." We believe the fullness of revelation has taken flesh in Jesus the Christ. But if we also believe that every person is created in God's image, then any hints we can glean about persons and especially about healthy persons can add to our reflections about the humanity we share and the humanity we build in ministry. If humanistic psychology reveals to us a humanity poised in readiness for self-actualization and self-transcendence, we can see that baptism simply celebrates and summons us to become what we already are: images of the Lord who in our very being are ready and open to respond to God's presence in us and share that presence in self-giving love. Here is the ultimate ground for ministry.

In its magnificent ode to the human which begins the *Constitution on the Church in the Modern World*, Vatican Council II summons us to the Christian humanism which creates hearts in tune with that ministry:

> The joys and the hopes, the griefs and anxieties of the men of this age, especially those who are poor or in any way afflicted, these too are the joys and the hopes, the griefs and anxieties of the followers of Christ. Indeed, nothing genuinely human fails to raise an echo in their hearts.

Created in God's image, grounded in self-transcendence and self-giving love, such hearts are ready to echo and resound in ministry.

Conversation Starters

Directions: Please clarify your responses to the following questions. You might use these responses both in formal group discussion and informal conversation.

1) Who most helps you "spend your buck" today?

2) Which three people helped you most in the past?

3) What are your three strongest "masculine" and your three strongest "feminine" traits?

4) To whom do you apply the term "minister"?

5) Of the human senses, which is your favorite?

6) What was your last powerful dream?

7) When was the last time you played a hunch?

8) What is your favorite piece of music?

9) What is your favorite painting?

10) Who are your heroes and heroines?

11) Who was the person who last suffered with you in a time of pain?

12) Did your life ever seem at a dead end?

13) How did your latest friendship begin?

Where I Stand

Reminder: Complete the following sentences before and after reading the chapter. Doing so *before* reading will help you write the chapter from your own experience. Doing so *after* reading may lead you to amend parts of the chapter or to change your own thoughts and feelings. This process will help you clarify where you stand and what you want to share with others.

1) When people talk of God's presence in me, I feel . . .

2) When people talk of God's presence in others, I feel . . .

3) My three greatest gifts are . . .

4) My three greatest weaknesses are . . .

5) During the past five years I have grown more confident about . . .

6) I am happiest when . . .

7) I am most discouraged when . . .

8) About the human image of God, I believe . . .

9) About the value of psychology for understanding my faith, I believe . . .

2 The Imagination of God

Where I Stand

1) I first remember experiencing God's presence as a child when . . .

2) As a young person, I deepened my faith through . . .

3) I most deeply felt God's absence when . . .

4) Today I find God's presence especially in . . .

5) I like the exchange of peace at Mass because . . .

6) I dislike the exchange of peace because . . .

7) I begin my prayer by . . .

8) About humankind as image of God, I believe . . .

We return to words about God. Words about man from the humanistic psychologists give some flesh to humans as the fruit of God's imagination. Now we need to clarify just what we mean when we say, "God imagines" (or when we say anything about God). We also need to ponder his presence in his images, for that will show us where to look for all the ministers of his presence.

Remember, all language about God is the language of analogy. We say that human beings have imagination, that we make images. We are not talking about the public relations kind of image-making which sells presidents and playboys. We speak rather of the gifts of imagining and dreaming and wondering and of the images which spring forth from imag-i-na-tion. We look at the human process of imagining. We look to our faith experience of God's presence in our lives. We look to the language that the people of the Judaeo-Christian tradition used about God's presence. And we find that, from Genesis through St. Paul, our people have said that the human process of imagination gives us an analogy to speak of God's imaging of us. God's creation of us is something like our creation of images. If we are going to speak that way, we need to establish the rules of the game, the limits of any language about God.

About Oyster-Talk and God-Talk

Robert Farrar Capon sets such limits in *Hunting the Divine Fox*, in a tale about an oyster and a rock. Once upon a time an oyster lived next to a rock at the bottom of the sea. The oyster loved to remind the rock that animal was superior to mineral. One day, in a fit of mineral liberation, the rock retorted, "You should hear how the starfish ridicule oysters who cannot move. They call you nothing more than a rock with a stomach and tell jokes about oysters as the butt of underwater humor."

Well, this sent the oyster into a state of profound depression. He thought he had been the climax and center of creation, and now he finds he is simply a joke among his fellow creatures of the deep. So he closed up his shell, stopped saying his Rosary and going to Mass, and cursed the day he was spawned as a seed oyster.

After some days in splendid isolation the sea water began to get cold, so in desperation he prayed as a Job among oysters and begged the Almighty to give his life dignity and meaning. The Almighty, much to his surprise, answered him and acknowledged that he was at the bottom of the scale of creation. "But something has to be there, or it spoils the whole effect." More surprising, the Almighty went on to tell stories of all kinds of creatures which can move even more than starfish—squirrels, basketball players, and the Almighty's absolute favorite, the prima ballerina.

After this exposure to wonders he had never seen, the oyster felt humbler, yet more elated, than before. He set himself to philosophizing about these mysteries. He constructed theories about prima ballerinas whom he had never seen:

> Starfish move; ballerinas move.
> Starfish are deadly to oysters.
> Are ballerinas deadly to oysters?

This was not clear and not "de fide," because the Almighty said ballerinas were beautiful. They might not be deadly to oysters. After many hours of this, the oyster relaxed, fascinated but tired, unable to define or solve all the mysteries of ballerinas. The sea water at least seemed refreshing again. Capon concludes with this Chinese proverb: "He who hammers at things over his head easily hits nail right on thumb."

Capon follows this story with a chapter entitled "Analogies," which begins "and he who hammers higher does it easier still." Literally that would mean, if you are an oyster talking about ballerinas or a human talking about God, watch your language! When talking of God whose Mystery far outdances even prima ballerinas, never forget that we speak only in analogy, story, poetry, parable, and *images*. When we speak of God as the great image-maker, that talk is not based on pure fantasy or wishful thinking unrelated to reality. It is grounded on the experience of Jews and Christians that God is present in human-kind and especially in Jesus. Therefore, we can speak of God as image-maker and ourselves as his images. We really experience something of his love and compassion and healing and presence in our very being.

We need continually to remind ourselves, however, that all this talk of God is itself grounded in our human capacity to create images. The power of images is that they give us some hint of the majesty of the Mystery we name God. Their limit is that they are always analo-gies, and they always hammer at a Mystery which is over our head and which cannot be captured in mere human words. Their danger is that we can begin to believe that we have defined the Mystery, that there is nothing more to say, and that this is the only way to say it. How often we experience that danger in those who club us into their "or-thodoxies" by insisting that their images from Scripture or their creeds from the Councils have "said it all"! In contrast, Thomas Aquinas re-tains the humility of oysters hammering over their heads: ". . . man reaches the highest point of his knowledge about God when he knows that he knows him not, inasmuch as he knows that which is God tran-scends whatsoever he conceives of him" (*De Pot.*, 7, 5, ad 14). Thomas dies muted, unable to say anymore, proclaiming that all he has written is straw, because he is overwhelmed by the Mystery of God.

This little volume conceives God as image-maker who calls hu-mans to minister by living up to their vocation to be images of his presence. Ministry is imaging God's love in various ways so that peo-ple may experience him as alive and well in our times. God is more than that. Ministry is more than that. This analogy is simply one way to reach for and experience the joy of that Mystery above our heads.

Images Are *SELF*-Expressions

If we pick up the analogy now and affirm that God's presence in the world and in humans is *something like* our presence in the products of our imagining, what vision does that offer us about being ministers of his presence?

We begin by describing the human process of imagination, with the help of William Lynch.

> [The imagination] is all the resources of man, all his faculties, his whole history, his whole life, and his whole heritage, all brought to bear upon the concrete world inside and outside himself, to form images of the world, and thus to find it, cope with it, shape it, even make it. The task of the imagination is to imagine the real. However, that might also very well mean making the real, making the world, for every image formed by everybody is an active, creative step, for good or for bad. . . . This is true of the image we have of a man, a woman, a child, birth, life, death, morning, night, food, friend, the enemy, the self, the human, the world as world. . . . These images are packed with experience, history, concepts, judgments, decisions, wishes, hopes, disappointments, love, and hate. And all this gets into the actual concrete, visible, audible, tactile stuff of our images. *Thus one cannot get closer to a man, nor can a man get closer to himself, than through his images.* [William Lynch, *Christ and Prometheus: A New Age for the Secular.* Notre Dame: University of Notre Dame Press, 1970, p. 23.]

As I understand him, Karl Rahner's use of the word "symbol" is close to Lynch's use of image. For Rahner, symbol (image) is our means of *self*-possession and *self*-expression. Notice both Lynch and Rahner insist that we are not over here and our images over there. No, *we* are *in our images.* Moreover, we are mysteries to ourselves. We shall never completely know ourselves. The older we get, the more we know there is to understand of self. What we know is our images of self. We come to *possess* a bit more of self, understand a bit more of self, by pondering our self-images. If I come to see myself as clown, or explorer, or prophet, or competitor, or martyr, or conformist, or dreamer, or wounded healer, I am drawing a bit closer to the me who will still be more than that. But I am getting some hints about me.

The same holds for others who would get to know me. For example, the longer and closer two people live together in love, the more they become mystery to each other. They know they cannot define the mystery of the other person. But in the intimacy of friendship or marriage, they share over the years countless *expressions* of their care and love — expressions which truly reveal the person imaged as lover, friend, teacher, consoler, rock of Gibraltar, or angel of mercy. When they ponder and draw close to these images, they are at intercourse with their very selves. Images are the entry point into the self. Notice Lynch's bottom line is this: we cannot get closer to other persons, nor to ourselves, than through our images.

Let us now push the analogy to God's relationship to his images. God is present in his images; they are his *Self*-expression, what Rahner calls his *Self*-communication. If our self-images are only hints about the mystery of the human person, so much more are God's images only hints of his Mystery which far surpasses our own. But the analogy affirms this: *we cannot get closer to God, nor can God get closer to himself, than through his images.* That is the affirmation to which all this talk of images has been leading. That affirmation proclaims, therefore, that there is no more pressing task for those who seek God than discerning his presence, his Self-communication, in his images.

For our purposes, we are interested more in how we come close to God in his images than in how God comes close to himself. In the interests of completeness, however, Rahner applies the analogy (as does Thomas Aquinas) consistently and asserts God gets close to himself and knows himself just as we do: in his Self-image. He speaks that image into a Word which is Son of God, unlike our self-images, complete, one with the Father, fully God.

Where do we draw near to God? Better, where does God draw near to us? He comes to us through that same Word in which he embodies all creation. Hebrews knew this. "By the Word of the Lord the heavens were made, their whole array by the breath of his mouth" (Ps. 33:6). Christians knew this. "In the beginning was the Word, and the Word was with God, and the Word was God. He was with God in the beginning. *All things were made through him, apart from him nothing was made*" (John 1:1-3). That Word is God's Self-image; God is present in his Word. That Word pours itself out in love and images itself in *all things* that have come to be. In this case, those images do not exhaust nor capture the Word. The Word will always have more to say. But in drawing close to all those images which the Word embodies, we draw close to God. This is why Thomas Aquinas can use another analogy. He says that God is related to the world as the human soul is related to the body. Just as the human body allows the human spirit to enter communion with the world, so all creation allows God to be present to us.

The World Is Image

First, God is present through the mystery and beauty of the entire universe. God speaks his Word, "Let there be . . ."; the universe is summoned out of chaos to be the sacred space of his presence. We draw close to nature, to light and darkness, sun and moon, water and living things in the waters, to land and vegetation and animals upon the land because in creation-evolution God first draws close to us.

This is true especially for the people of the natural sciences who ponder the mysteries of the universe. Although some scientists have not heard the news, for many other scientists and people of faith the old war between religious belief and science is over. Science does not describe why the world comes to be, but in part it seeks how the world comes to be. In so doing, it does not discover God through microscope or test tube; but science can bring persons face to face with wonder and mystery. In that confrontation they can step beyond science into religious faith.

The wonders of the universe can bring not only scientists but all of us into the sacred ground of mystery and beauty. I live in the most unchurched state in the nation, the state of Washington. Some suggest the problem (and for some, the blessing) is that the environment is the church. When one wakes up each (cloud-free) morning to the majesty of Mt. Rainier, one has no difficulty seeing why Jews experienced God on mountains. We have done some studies about where and when people in Seattle identify their experiences of God, and the number who find God in nature is significantly larger in the Pacific Northwest than it is in "beautiful downtown Chicago." Because God images himself in nature, we can paraphrase St. John: God is beauty, and he who lives in beauty lives in God and God in him.

Humankind Is Image

We draw close to man/woman, to all humankind, for there is where the Word begins to climax. Notice the language of Genesis: "Let us make man in our image, after our likeness . . . so God created man in his own image, in the image of God he created him" (Gen. 2:7, 1:26-27). Man/woman image the divine. Let's play with another analogy. In friendship and marriage two persons are present to each other, drawing forth the best from each other, entering deeply through self-giving love into the life of each other, so that each can say, "You are within me, always present to me." Yet, they do not become each other. Healthy friendships do not devour persons. Each person remains unique, in fact, more unique than before because the loved one has summoned forth the best in him or her.

This analogy suggests that this is how it is between God and every person. God is present as lover to every person; and, as in every healthy friendship, each lover blossoms. The human person becomes more uniquely himself or herself, more free, more creative, more alive, more loving. But in a sense God also becomes more himself, more revealed as present in the beloved, summoning to freedom, creativity, life, and love. When believers see life and love present in the human person, in faith they can begin to see the God who *is* life and love imaged there.

That can be true of every person in whom we discover freedom, life, and love, members of every religious tradition and also non-believers who dedicate themselves to building a more just and humane world. Christian believers will not force their beliefs on non-believers, but secretly and quietly Christians can rejoice in and marvel about all the people in whom they see God's presence. That should be especially true for Catholic Christians who are Catholic because they are catholic, because they have returned to the meaning of that word in the sense that they believe in God's universal presence in all humankind.

Israel Is Image

In our tradition, we draw close especially to the people of Israel, because in our faith it is there that we see God's Word received and imaged with special power. We see there persons who do what God does, persons who express themselves, give of themselves, image themselves in a self-giving love which propels them into journey and Exodus: Abraham, uprooted and called into a new future with no AAA insurance and no *National Geographic* map; Moses summoned into the desert to "let my people go"; David empowered to build justice; Isaiah touched by fire; Jeremiah called out of his youth to promise a new covenant, written on hearts; Mary blessed among women because she let it be done to her according to God's Word. The whole nation, Israel, throughout its history—an example to us of how a people can journey from sin to fidelity and from horrible evil and genocide to renewed hope when they come to believe in the enduring and faithful presence of God.

Jesus Is Image

In our Christian faith we draw even closer to Jesus because there God's Word reaches its crescendo. There "the Word became flesh and made his dwelling among us" (John 1:14). There is "the image of the invisible God" (Col. 1:15).

Note: Jesus is not the first image. Jesus is not the first in whom the Word became flesh. In our faith, Jesus is the "Image of images," the Word received and proclaimed as never before or since, a Word which has become, in Rahner's words, "the poetry of God our Father," the enfleshment of his wildest dreams, his delightful wonder, his most vivid imagination. The Word had been imaging God in flesh from the beginning: in the universe, in humankind, in Israel. But never before or since has a man, "like us in everything except sin," so imaged the self-giving love of God for sinners, the poor, the lost, the outcast. On the Cross, especially, Christians see the history of God imaging his love for us and a man imaging his love for God and us reach its unsurpassed climax. This is what God can be. This is what persons can be if they allow God's love to be present in their lives. Only God could make this man. One cannot get closer to God than through this image.

The Church Is Image

Finally, Christians draw close to each other because the climactic moment of Jesus resounds in us. Jesus has poured forth his Spirit upon us. Jesus has enlivened us with the Good News of his presence in us. Jesus calls us to let God's self-giving love do in us what it has done in him. Jesus calls us to experience his Father's love imaged all around us in the world, in persons, in himself, in ourselves. That is the Christian vocation. Christian ministry is imaging God's love and presence so that others might do the same.

T. H. White wrote a delightful story about how God creates us— a story which gives us another picture of how God sends us on our way to minister.

> [In the beginning God] called the embryos before Him, and saw that they were good. Perhaps I ought to explain, . . . that all embryos look very much the same. . . . The embryos stood in front of God, with their feeble hands clasped politely over their stomachs . . . and God addressed them. He said, "Now, you embryos, here you are, all looking exactly the same, and We are going to give you the choice of what you want to be. . . . You may alter any parts of yourselves into anything which you think would be useful to you in later life. . . ."
>
> All the embryos thought the matter over politely, and then, one by one, they stepped up before the eternal throne. . . . Some chose to use their arms as flying machines and their mouths as weapons, or crackers, or drillers, or spoons, while others selected to use their bodies as boats and their hands as oars. . . . The asking and granting took up two long days—they were the fifth and sixth, so far as I remember—and at the very end of the sixth day, just before it was time to knock off for Sunday, they had got through all the little embryos except one. This embryo was Man.
>
> "Well, Our little man," said God. "You have waited till the last, and slept on your decision, . . . What can We do for you?"
>
> "Please, God," said the embryo, "I think that You made me in the shape which I now have for reasons best known to Yourselves, and that it would be rude to change. If I am to have my choice I will stay as I am. . . . I will stay a defenceless embryo all my life, doing my best to make myself a few feeble implements out of the wood, iron, and the other materials which You have seen fit to put before me. . . ."
>
> "Well done," exclaimed the Creator in delighted tones. "Here, all you embryos, come here with your beaks and whatnots to look upon Our first Man. He is the only one

who has guessed Our riddle, out of all of you, and We have great pleasure in conferring upon him the Order of Dominion over the Fowls of the Air, and the Beasts of the Earth, and the Fishes of the Sea. . . . As for you, Man, you will be a naked tool all your life, though a user of tools. You will look like an embryo till they bury you, but all the others will be embryos before your might. Eternally undeveloped, you will always remain potential in Our image, able to see some of Our sorrows and to feel some of Our joys. We are partly sorry for you, Man, but partly hopeful. Run along then, and do your best. And listen, Man, before you go . . ."

"Well?" asked Adam, turning back from his dismissal.

"We were only going to say," said God shyly, twisting Their hands together, "Well, We were just going to say, God bless you." [T. H. White, *The Once and Future King.* New York: Berkley Publishing Corporation, 1939, pp. 191-193.]

Conversation Starters

1) What images best describe you?

2) What images best describe the person you love most?

3) What are your favorite images or analogies which describe God?

4) What are your least favorite descriptions of God?

5) When did you last sense God's presence in nature?

6) When did you last sense God's presence in someone not of your religious faith?

7) Who is your favorite person in the Old Testament?

8) Do you have any Jewish friends? If so, what do you learn from them?

9) What is your favorite title or name for Jesus?

10) Who is your favorite Christian saint?

11) Have Church people ever made it more difficult for you to find God?

12) What living Christians most reveal God's presence to you?

Where I Stand

1) I first remember experiencing God's presence as a child when . . .

2) As a young person, I deepened my faith through . . .

3) I most deeply felt God's absence when . . .

4) Today I find God's presence especially in . . .

5) I like the exchange of peace at Mass because . . .

6) I dislike the exchange of peace because . . .

7) I begin my prayer by . . .

8) About humankind as image of God, I believe . . .

3 Jesus: The Image of God

Where I Stand

1) I wonder if Jesus . . .

2) I wonder why Jesus . . .

3) I wonder what Jesus would do if . . .

4) When the Bible says, "God speaks to us," I wonder . . .

5) The most important community in my life is . . .

6) At most celebrations of Mass I feel . . .

7) About people on welfare I feel . . .

8) I believe Jesus receives from his Father . . .

9) I believe Jesus gives to us . . .

In our faith, the one sent by the Father who "did his best," the one most blessed by God is Jesus the Christ. God is most alive and well in Jesus, *the* image of the invisible God (cf. Col 1).

In our times it has not always been so. I have been in priestly ministry for sixteen years, and during those years the cover stories of *Time* magazine give a capsule history and medical report on the health of Jesus and his Father in the last half of the twentieth century.

April 8, 1966, the week after Easter, *Time* featured a deadly black cover on which was emblazoned in huge red letters, "IS GOD DEAD?" Those were the years of the "death of God" theologians who announced the demise of a deity upon whom humans had been childishly dependent and the resurrection of "man come of age" who was ready to claim responsibility for his life.

December 26, 1969, during Christmas week, there were rumors of a sudden, miraculous recovery of the dead deity (and also hope for the faith of the editors of *Time*) because that week, on a white cover with yellow sunbursts, in huge blue letters, our friendly weekly news-magazine asked the question, "IS GOD COMING BACK TO LIFE?" And there was more joy in heaven over one *Time* magazine that re-pented than over ninety-nine *Our Sunday Visitors* which had no need of repentance!

June 21, 1971—there was a new springtime and resurrection for the Lord was now not only up and walking but dancing down the streets with the Jesus people and celebrating in huge football stadiums with "born again" Christians. On the cover that week, *Time* featured a quasi-psychedelic portrait of Jesus topped by a rainbow proclaim-ing "THE JESUS REVOLUTION."

Religious folk might take heart that our leader is getting better press until we begin to do a more thorough examination on just who the Jesus is who has come back to life. Who is your Christ? That 1971 issue of *Time*, for example, quoted an evangelist who said that for many young people Jesus is the authority figure their fathers aren't. Jesus is a source of law and order, of discipline, an answer-giver. Peo-ple who were lost, who perhaps had been strung out on drugs, could join well-disciplined communities and carry around in their pocket the biblical answer-book of this Jesus who provided quick formulae for all questions. Certainly, Jesus gives us a vision of life. But that same Bible seems to present him as a fellow participant in the human adven-ture, with questions and temptations, not just for forty days in the desert but all his life. Didn't he die asking a question, "Why have you abandoned me?" This is a man who, far from having all the answers, seems able to live and die with the questions because his final word is one of trust in the Father—"Father, into your hands I commit my spirit!"

Who is your Jesus? A study of Lutherans in the late 1960s con-cluded that in practice most Lutherans had teamed up with those ancient heretics, the Monophysites (in Greek, literally "one-nature"); Jesus has one nature and it is divine. The Monophysites couldn't be-lieve that God would dirty himself with messy and depraved and sinful human nature. Jesus was obviously God, so he couldn't be man.

A pastor recently told me a story of a contemporary Catholic Monophysite. He had been assigned to a parish in which the former pastor had done almost nothing to live out the vision of Vatican II; this was especially true of the parish liturgies, which remained "divine," distant, deadly, and deadening. The new pastor came in and simply followed the new directions for Mass. We are now encouraged to greet people warmly, smile, communicate, and act like human beings who have not lost our personalities to some human-hating God. The priest proceeded to follow these rubrics, and in a few weeks received a letter with the following complaint: "If God wanted us to act like human beings at Mass, he would have become a man!" Precisely, my dear Monophysite! Another pastor told me of a similar complaint which came in the mail: "If Jesus knew what was going on in this parish, he'd turn over in his grave!" With those two letters, there goes Christmas, and there goes Easter! That's a real "Jesus revolution!"

Who is your Jesus? On the other hand, in more recent days the predominant heresy seems to be new Arians, not Monophysites. Arians also found humanity depraved and unworthy of God. Jesus was obviously a man; so Arians concluded he couldn't be God. They made him a kind of demi-god—neither fish nor fowl.

Contemporary Arians sometimes present Jesus as just one more "good guy." He becomes a good example for us, just like our other favorite heroes and heroines—John Kennedy, Mother Teresa, Martin Luther King, or John XXIII. The Jesus who says, "He who sees me sees the Father"; the Jesus who speaks not only in God's name but who announces God's Kingdom in his own name by saying, "*I* say to you"; the Jesus whom Scripture clearly presents as uniquely Saviour, God's Presence in the world, and God's Son, has become trivialized and banalized in such quasi-Arian folk ditties as "Jesus is just all right with me!" In part, he was crucified by our predecessors because he proclaimed both the judgment and the Good News of God which they could not hear and which was not "just all right" with them. Who is your Jesus?

Jesus—Revelation of the Father

In the faith of the biblical writers, God did get messed up with the human through the flesh and blood of Jesus, much to the consternation of Monophysites and Arians. God is so much present in the humanity of Jesus and Jesus so much does what God does that they proclaim him Son of God.

For Greeks, talk of sonship evokes thoughts about abstract natures and essences. We grew up with that Greek approach, hallowed at the Council of Chalcedon in the fifth century, which gave us a Jesus with two natures and one Person (notice, no human person but only the divine person of the Son of God, using a Greek notion of person). For Hebrews, however, talk of sonship speaks more of concrete existence and living like the Father. "If I am not doing my Father's work, there is no need to believe me; but if I am doing it, then even if you refuse to believe in me, at least believe in the work I do; then you will know for sure that the Father is in me and I am in the Father" (John 10:36-38). To be a Son is to image the life of the Father. "Philip, how long have you been with me and you do not know that he who sees me sees the Father?" (John 14:9).

The mission of Jesus, then, is to let the Good News out: to reveal the Father's presence in the world by doing what his Father does. The God who has been present to all humankind from the beginning has been calling persons to image his love, and people have been searching for those images and asking what God is like. As Leonard Bernstein's character sings in *Mass*, the question is not so much, "Do I believe in God?" but "Does God believe in me?" The God imaged in Jesus turns out to believe in us more than we dreamed. John Shea, in *The Challenge of Jesus*, says that the God present in Jesus Christ is not so much Francis Thompson's "hound of heaven" but a bulldog, more stubborn and stiff-necked than his stiff-necked people, who holds on to us for dear life in his relentless pursuit of life for us and life to the full (cf. John 10:10). God present in Jesus turns out to be more than any of us could ever have imaged or imagined.

Jesus—God Giving, Man Receiving, Man Giving What He Received

How does Jesus proclaim this Good News for us? In an insightful article entitled "The Incarnation: God's Giving and Man's Receiving," published in *Horizons*, Vol. I, Donald Gray suggests that in Jesus we see God giving, man receiving, and man giving what he has received. How the divine and human are present in Jesus will always remain one of those mysteries over our heads. For the most part, we have hammered at that mystery with Greek tools of nature and person which

Gray finds abstract and static. He says we should speak in the more dynamic and interpersonal categories of actions rather than natures. That brings to mind Buckminster Fuller's declaration that for him God is more verb than noun. The actions which Gray chooses are giving and receiving.

First, in Jesus we see God giving. We have already reflected upon a God who has been giving, creating, loving, and letting-be from the beginning. "God is love" (John 4:8), and love at its root is a mystery of self-giving, of letting-be, of giving to another so that the other can be. In Jesus, God acts in a way wholly consistent with how he has always acted, except that he outdoes himself in giving. He gives fully of his Spirit to this man and fills him to the brim. Jesus is overwhelmed by the presence of his Father's Spirit; and, for his inaugural address, Luke has Jesus quote Isaiah: "The Spirit of the Lord is upon me . . ." (Luke 4:16) so that the blind, the lame, the leper, the captive, the poor will know the healing and self-giving love of God.

Second, in Jesus we also see a man receiving. In his humanity, Jesus knows he is no self-made man. He receives everything from the Father. Too often, with an emphasis on divinity in Jesus, we have made this man who understood his total dependence on his Father into a Superman who avoided the pain of the human adventure.

Remember how that serial began:

> Faster than a speeding bullet. More powerful than a loco-motive. Able to leap tall buildings with a single bound. It's Superman! Strange visitor from another planet, who came to earth with powers and abilities far beyond those of mortal men, and who, disguised as Clark Kent, mild-mannered reporter for a great metropolitan newspaper, fights a never-ending battle for truth, justice, and the American Way.

Robert Capon, in *Hunting the Divine Fox*, insists, "If that isn't popular christology, I'll eat my hat!" No grappling with the mystery of God's presence in Jesus can be resolved by destroying his humanity. The humanity which the New Testament resoundingly attributes to Jesus is that of a vigorously assertive man who was tempted, questioned life, and searched out its meaning. In Jesus we see that even when a man is open to receiving the love of God, he does not escape rejection, fear, weariness, loneliness, or the cross. This is no Superman who can leap into a phone booth, climb into his Easter clothes, and bound back to the planet heaven freed from the pain of the human journey. No, in the midst of darkness and death this man trusts a God who would not let a life like his come to a dead end. In the midst of death this man receives resurrection.

In a letter to Jesuit ordinands, Michael Buckley speaks of the human Jesus beset by weakness (cf. Hebrews 2:18; 4:15; 5:2) who is absolutely dependent on the Father and receives everything from the Father. He contrasts the deaths of Socrates and Jesus. Socrates died with grace and poise. He satisfied himself about evidence for life after death, found no cause for fear, drank the poison and died. A real classy exit! And Jesus sweat blood, almost hysterical with terror and fear. He turned with anguish to his friends for comfort and support and prayed to escape death. He cried his final question out of his emptiness, "My God, why have you abandoned me?" Socrates—one of the most heroic men who ever lived—died a philosopher. Jesus of Nazareth—suffering, abandoned, frightened, a more profoundly weak and poor man, more wounded by human rejection and contempt, more touched by human love and hate—died a saviour.

This is an image of human self-transcendence that we do not find affirmed with such power in the humanistic psychologists. Those who would continue, touched by the Spirit of Jesus to image God, will see that God was most present to a man when that man was most empty, most open, most dependent, most weak, most receptive. Here is a faith-vision of the human which goes beyond Maslow, which proclaims that, when humanity is most empty, it is precisely then that God can fill us with life. We see that in Jesus—the man receiving.

Finally, in Jesus we see a man giving what he has received. Jesus gives to others the gifts he has received from his Father. Always called by his Father into the future, in the present Jesus gives us hints of the shape of that future: unbounded mercy for sinners, healing for the sick in body and spirit, thanksgiving meals and wedding banquets for all who receive and rejoice in the gifts of God, reconciliation and "shalom" for this fragmented human family of ours. He has the kingdom of God ever before him, and he becomes the "man for others," the Servant of Yahweh, the man on a mission of giving as God gives. The rest of this chapter elaborates on what Jesus has to give. Gray, in the article cited previously in this chapter, summarizes Jesus' mission as Saviour in these terms of giving and receiving:

Jesus becomes Saviour for us when he enables a new life by freeing us to receive what God is giving. Jesus saves when he sends us into our own lives to discover there the same divine giving at work as in his own. Jesus saves when we begin to receive in his spirit what he received and to give in his spirit what he gave.

The Mission and Ministries of Jesus

That brings us to reflect on the ministries of Jesus, which must be the starting point for all Christian ministries. In a sense, we should think of one mission and many ministries. Jesus is sent by the Father to reveal the Good News of God's presence to human life in the present and future, offering resurrection to those who will receive the gift of God. This is his *mission*.

Over the years, those who have pondered the Jesus of the New Testament have discerned various ways in which Jesus invited people to experience God's presence. We might call these *ministries*, since we have described ministries as the many ways in which the human images God's presence in care and service. Discerning the ministries of Jesus will be the key to the ministries to which he calls his followers.

A number of Scriptural exegetes and theologians have suggested four fundamental ministries which have their roots in the Good News which Jesus in the New Testament brings as image of God: ministry of the Word (*kerygma*), ministry of community-building (*koinonia*), ministry of celebrating (*leiturgia*), and ministry of serving-healing (*diakonia*). The National Catechetical Directory, *Sharing the Light of Faith*, also identified these four ministries as the four components (no. 39), or purposes (no. 227), or dimensions (no. 215) of catechesis. Can we discern in Jesus the beginnings of these ministries which have subsequently taken multiple forms in the lives of his followers?

The Ministry of the Word

Both Old and New Testaments reveal a God who speaks to his people. This is no remote, silent, unapproaching and unapproachable monarch akin to some oriental potentate. No, this is the God who draws near, who participates in human history, whose Word leads to freedom through the events of Exodus and to resurrection through the event of Jesus.

Notice, theologians like to talk about the "event" of Jesus, even the Word-event of Jesus. They are trying to be faithful to the Jewish meaning of "word" (*dabar*) which would be better translated "word-deed." Jewish words are sacramental, i.e., they effect what they signify. When Hebrews name something, they act through their words and determine the very being of things. A Jew cannot take back his word or the name because they have already changed the world.

God's Word acts like that. "Yes, as the rain and the snow come down from the heavens and do not return without watering the earth, making it yield and giving growth to provide seed for the sower and bread for the eating, so the Word that goes from my mouth does not return to me empty, without carrying out my will and succeeding in what it was sent to do" (Isa. 55:10-11). That is the Word-deed that becomes flesh in Jesus.

Jesus' first message, then, is not his preaching but his entire life. The saving self-communication of God becomes flesh in the self-giving love of this man poured out in sight for the blind, forgiveness for sinners, compassion for the poor, and in body broken and blood shed on the Cross. Jesus' ministry of the Word is first of all a story, his life story, his word-deed, his *dabar*.

In this sense, Jesus himself is also the great Parable. Parables in the narrower sense are stories which build to a climax which usually jolts the hearer, challenges the conventional wisdom, throws a curve. Well, the curve thrown by God in the Parable-deed of Jesus' life is that life comes out of death, self-actualization out of self-emptying, Easter out of Calvary.

In many other ways Jesus is the prophet of God's Word, the preacher who speaks the Word of the Lord with authority. For our purposes, I want to stress only one of those ways: Jesus as the teller of tales. St. Paul may spin theologies; Jesus continues to spin yarns. Historical and critical studies of Scripture indicate that many of the gospels' parables did originate with Jesus, perhaps in slightly different form. These stories dramatically present a God who overpays workers in the vineyard, who scurries around looking for lost coins and sheep, who runs down the road to embrace a wandering son, in other words, a God better than many of us imagine.

Later, we shall reflect on the implications of Jesus' ministry of the Word for us. For now, let us just say that many of us may flounder in speaking about God, but all of us have a *dabar*—a "word-deed" that speaks to others louder than words. Our ministry of the Word will most often be to let that "word-deed" speak Good News to people who will respond far better to lives offered to them than to words alone.

Also, we may not be scientific theologians, but we all have a personal story of faith to tell, especially our journeys through death to resurrection. In that sense, every Christian can be minister of God's Word.

The Ministry of Community-Building

Basic to the Judaeo-Christian experience of God is the experience of covenant which gathers a people. The source of this community is not the people but the Lord who initiates the covenant, who chooses the Jews as the least of all people to be his special possession (cf. Deut. 7:6-9), who promises a deepening of the covenant to be written on their hearts which will give them one heart (cf. Jer. 32:37-41), fulfilling that promise through the broken body and shed blood of Jesus, who dies that all people may be one just as Jesus and his Father are one (cf. John 17:20-21).

How does the ministry of Jesus image God the builder of covenants? He insists that the relationship with God is the first word to be said about covenants and that the Law is always in second place. With the good Jew, he affirms that God's free and loving choice of his people comes first, and then come the responsibilities of living the law of love in return. In other words, unlike the legalists in both Judaism and Christianity, he gently reveals to a woman caught in adultery, a tax collector not above a little chicanery, and a thief on a cross, that the overriding criterion for entrance into the covenant is *the simple acceptance of God's mercy*. That is the Good News which breaks down élite barriers to community and welcomes leper and blind man, poor and sinner, Jew and Gentile. That is the Good News we find so hard to believe—that God's people includes us.

Jesus also deepens the bonds of union. The covenant is now written not just on stone tablets but, as Jeremiah promised, on converted hearts which have received the Good News and extend it to others. The so-called "others" are now one in heart. What we share with the hungry, the thirsty, the stranger, the naked, and the prisoner, we share with Jesus (cf. Matt. 25:31-46). All of this is possible because the Father is in Jesus and Jesus in the Father, and all people who are united in their spirit are one with one another (cf. John 17).

Jesus also unites a people not just as friends or fellowship groups.

That which primarily draws this people together is their focus and expectation of the kingdom of God set before them. We hear much complaint these days that large groups cannot be communities. In response, we hear complaints from sociologists that religious communities use that word too loosely, since there are different levels of community. Some sociologists suggest that large groups of people can still draw together at one level of community *if* they are committed to shared values, ideals, dreams, to a common purpose and direction toward the future. I often think of the thousands of people at Lourdes, or St. Peter's Square, or at large religious congresses in the United States. Unlike the weekend evening Mass crowd in many parishes who come with little purpose, they sing and pray enthusiastically because they are united in seeking God's kingdom.

Scriptural scholars agree that, more than anything else, Jesus' expectation and commitment to God's coming kingdom dominated his message. Most also agree that Jesus did not "found" a Church in the usual sense of the word. He did bring to life an expectation among his followers that his Father was coming now and would come in the future with his kingship of love and mercy. When that final coming was delayed, those followers began a Church. But what binds that Church together in community is not simply friendship and fellowship but shared faith and commitment to Jesus' dreams about the present and future coming of the reign of God.

The Ministry of Celebration

The Old Testament proclaims that the Word at God's side when he created the heavens and earth was a playful, delightful Word. "Then was I beside him as his craftsman, and I was his delight day by day, playing before him all the while, playing on the surface of his earth; and I found delight in the sons of men" (Prov. 8:30-31).

When that Word becomes flesh to image that same God, he insists, "Do not look dismal" (Matt. 6:16). He lets the oil be poured on him in anointing; and he and his disciples do not fast because, after all, the bridegroom is here, and it is time to rejoice.

Jesus' ministry of celebration is not primarily one of founding rituals as a Jewish cultic priest. Although the Letter to the Hebrews, late in the New Testament writings, calls him high priest in his resurrection, during his life he is not a member of the Jewish institutional priesthood. His ministry is rather his call to thanks-giving, to Eucharist for Good News. Rejoice—the coin is found, the lost sheep is home. Stop your toil—you're invited to a banquet. Zacchaeus, get out of that tree—let's have dinner at your place. Give thanks—all you latecomers to the vineyard will be overpaid. And, perhaps most consoling of all, my son, my son, put on this ring, these sandals, this fine robe—let's kill the fatted calf and throw a party.

Jesus calls all Christians to celebrate all the ways in which God offers life to people.

The Ministry of Serving-Healing

In a sense, all ministries are service. *Diakonia* marks especially in Jesus the quality of Suffering Servant, wounded healer, fellow traveler into our dark nights of fear and loneliness, hanging on the Cross with us when we feel most weak and empty. The classic texts are in Hebrews: "For because he himself has suffered and been tempted, he is able to help those who are tempted. . . . For we have not a high priest who is unable to sympathize with our weaknesses, but one who in every respect has been tempted as we are, yet without sinning. . . . He can deal gently with the ignorant and wayward since he himself is beset with weakness" (Hebrews 2:18; 4:15; 5:2).

Rejoicing is one pole of Christ, suffering is the other. As Suffering Servant who knows our wounds from the inside, he has compassion for (literally, he can "feel with") the hurts and struggles and the pain of his brothers and sisters. He has wept over Jerusalem when rejected. He has tried to gather the chicks under his wings, and they wouldn't have him. When he was most like his Father and forgave the adulteress and ate with tax collectors and sinners, he was ridiculed and expelled for such bad taste. He has healed the blind and been accused of working by the powers of evil. Most of all, he has died our death. We have, therefore, a God present in human flesh who has cried our tears and felt our abandonment. Nothing can ever be the same again.

Jesus as Suffering Servant and wounded healer also illumines two qualities of ministry which his followers too easily forget. First, authority in the Church—does that not sometimes bring to mind images of domination, raw power, demands for blind obedience, the pomp and circumstance of secular rulers in all their regal splendor? Authority in Jesus—does that not bring to mind intimate union with his Father, wisdom, the power to author new life, healing, forgiveness, conversion, not because he lords it over us but because "he has been there," one with us, the authority of knowing us from the inside? He is the Son of Man who has no place to lay his head (Luke 9:58), and he forever asks his followers if they can drink that cup with him. If so, they must serve as he has served. "Anyone among you who aspires to greatness must serve the rest, and whoever wants to rank first among you must serve the needs of all" (Matt. 20:26-27).

Second, Jesus who is "beset by weakness" and allows God to be present through his emptiness and powerlessness challenges us to ask, "Just who are the ministers?" Are they only the "professionals," the institutional folks who get ordained, installed, commissioned and even paid to minister? Jesus ministered from his weakness and from outside the institutions of his time. Jesus served from the margins of his people, and often his compelling concerns were to be with the other marginal people—sinners, the poor, the crippled, the lost and wandering, the little ones (in biblical terms, the *anawim*). Jesus' ministry of service not only challenges his followers to outreach, to move beyond churchly concerns and institutions, but also to remember who will do the ministry of healing. It will often be those with the most wounds who know best what healing means. It will be the *anawim* of our times, those who like Jesus "can deal gently with the ignorant and wayward since they themselves are beset by weakness." Dan Berrigan once said that the poor have it hard, and the hardest thing they have is those who are more fortunate. Do we allow the poor to minister as the poor Jesus did?

The next four chapters will round out these four dimensions of ministry in the life of Jesus' followers today. The final chapter will trace the history of ministries in the Church and address the controversy about how broad an application the term "ministry" should have. If any form of ministry, however, is to deserve the name Christian, its launching pad must in some way be Jesus the Word, the builder of community, that great cause of our joy and celebration, the servant-healer. The Risen Christ still lives to share Good News, initiate new covenants of mercy and love, welcome us back home and throw parties, and heal our most gaping wounds. He pours out his Spirit upon us that we might do the same.

Conversation Starters

1) Do you believe Jesus has all the answers for our problems?

2) Do you believe Jesus is primarily a good example of how to live?

3) Do you believe Jesus always knew how things were going to turn out?

4) Do you believe Jesus liked some people more than others?

5) Is there a time when your life spoke louder than your words?

6) Can you tell of a time when you experienced death and then a resurrection to new life?

7) What makes you feel part of a community?

8) Has someone ever made you feel undeserving when he or she forgave you?

9) For what are you most grateful?

10) Have you ever enjoyed being dismal and letting others know it?

11) Do you really believe that Jesus in his own life has experienced the kinds of fears and pains you find in yours?

12) What do you hear when you hear the word "authority"?

13) Can you tell of a time when you set out to help someone and they ended up helping you?

Where I Stand

1) I wonder if Jesus . . .

2) I wonder why Jesus . . .

3) I wonder what Jesus would do if . . .

4) When the Bible says, "God speaks to us," I wonder . . .

5) The most important community in my life is . . .

6) At most celebrations of Mass I feel . . .

7) About people on welfare I feel . . .

8) I believe Jesus receives from his Father . . .

9) I believe Jesus gives to us . . .

4 Ministries of the Word

Where I Stand

1) My knowledge of God and Jesus is . . .

2) The most important question for me about my life right now is . . .

3) When it comes to expressing my feelings, I usually . . .

4) The person in the gospels most like me is . . .

5) I feel our nation is . . .

6) My favorite teacher was . . .

7) The best homily I ever heard was . . .

8) My favorite poem is . . .

9) The priest who has most touched my life is . . .

A Dutch priest, Henri Nouwen, tells a story which will serve to launch our discussion of ministries of the Word. A sculptor was chipping away at a huge block of marble. A little boy watched him work for many weeks until, finally, he was amazed to see that the sculptor had created a beautiful marble lion. The little boy ran up to the sculptor with eyes wide with wonder, and he exclaimed, "Hey, Mister, how did you know there was a lion hidden in that rock?"

Nouwen comments that long before he knows the marble, the sculptor has to know the lion. He has to imagine the lion. He has to know the lion "by heart." The most pressing question for a sculptor, therefore, is, "How many things do you know by heart?" If he knows magnificent women and men, he will discover them in the marble. If he knows God by heart, he will find God in the marble.

The most pressing question for a Christian minister of the Word is also, "Do you know God and Jesus and yourself and God's people by heart?" We have discussed ministry as imaging God's presence, as a feat of "Imag-i-na-tion" through which we come to know God "by heart" at the very center of our lives, and then image in word and deed his message of Good News and his saving love. To know God by heart, however, also means that we need to know ourselves and other people by heart.

Ministers of the Word, then, are all those who have heard God's Word, who have come to faith that it is a healing Word which brings life out of death, and who share that faith with others. This includes far more than the formal ministries of preaching and teaching. It includes all believers who have searched out the meaning of life and have grappled with the pain and grandeur of being human. They have heard the dictum of Socrates that "the unexamined life is not worth living." These believers have struggled with the life-and-death questions which emerge from an examined life. What is a good man? What is a good woman? To what destiny are we called? To what shall I be loyal? These people of faith have come to believe in a Presence which they call God, which speaks a Word about goodness and our future and a cause worthy of our loyalty. Like Jesus, who died asking a question (Why have you abandoned me?), these people of faith do not let life trample over them, and they do not blindly accept someone else's answers. They are vigorously assertive people who, with Rainer Maria Rilke, have learned "to love the questions themselves while waiting for and working out the answers" and who have personally experienced the Word of life.

That is why they have come to know by heart and not just by head. No abstract philosophizing here. No theologies fussing over how many angels can perch on the head of a pin. No cold and clanking theorizing aimed at pure logic and objectivity. No, their word of faith has emerged from their personal pilgrimage through death to life, from their passionate quest for meaning in the midst of guilt, loneliness, weariness, frustration and hurt. In the midst of this pilgrimage they speak a word which sometimes falters and stammers yet is nonetheless an encouraging word of faith that life is for us and that nothing can separate us from the love of God in Christ Jesus (cf. Rom. 8).

To proclaim that Word well calls for special gifts of imagination.

In an earlier chapter quoting William Lynch, imagination was described as all our resources, all our faculties, our whole history, our whole life, and our whole heritage, all brought to bear upon the world to form images. "These images are packed with experience, history, concepts, judgments, decisions, wishes, hopes, disappointments, love, and hate." After all, we are speaking from the heart, forming images of ourselves, our people, and our God whom we know by heart. Our words of faith, therefore, will not be so much the language of logic or analysis but rather the language of image and symbol, story and poem.

Psychologists distinguish between primary process thinking and secondary process thinking. The former is the thinking we do in our heart, with our intuitions and feelings, with our imagination. It is also called left-handed thinking, arising from the left side of our personality and our body which some claim is controlled by the right lobe of the brain. This is the source of gut-level reactions, of our most creative efforts in art and poetry, of hunches and lucky guesses, of our reflection on those things we feel most deeply.

Secondary process thinking is one step removed from our primary experiences. Where left-handed thinking deals with the inner world of feeling, the unconscious, mystery and eternity, right-handed thinking deals with the outer world of space and time, conscious life, logic, reason, and analysis. Left-handed thinking creates stories about our fears and hopes during times when we face those ultimate questions of death and life. Right-handed thinking produces theologies which systematically critique and analyze the meaning of those stories.

We need both types of thinking. In a reaction to the scientism of the first three quarters of this century, truth is now presumed to reside in your guts, your glands, and your stars; everywhere but in your cortex. Some of the most exciting movements in the Church have been tarnished by this cult of anti-reason, and some "encountered" couples and pentecostal types of charismatics have become more infallible than the pope about a Word of God which they have felt in their guts. We need right-handed thinkers, theologians, ministers of the Word who confront us with the wisdom of other people, keep us in touch with a Church tradition, and critique and analyze our stories of faith to help us hear a Word from God which is more than feelings erupting from our guts and perhaps our gastric acidity.

Having said that, I want to affirm, nonetheless, that most of us will be ministers of the Word through tapping our resources of primary experience, left-handed thinking, imagination, and our language of the heart. Most of us will not be professional theologians or even classroom teachers. But if we are believers, all of us have a faith to share and a story to tell as ministers of God's Word which we have come to know by heart. The rest of this chapter will discuss six ministries of the Word, all of which call for profound left-handed thinking. The list is not exclusive; these are simply six ministries which speak God's Word from a deeply personal experience of faith grounded in primary experience. These ministries are: story-tellers, prophets, educators, preachers, poets, and priests.

Story-Tellers

As I mentioned earlier, St. Paul spins theologies from his right hand. Jesus remains a southpaw who tells tales. The art of story-telling is more than just a gift of gab. With Jesus, we can see that stories which really touch people and move them to put themselves into the story are those which arise from persons who have been participants in the human adventure. They have searched life for meaning and have faced life and death issues. Therefore, they express their faith-response to life through stories which reveal that they know themselves and their God by heart. Their words are truly *dabar*, word-deeds that they have lived. Jesus speaks of prodigal sons and daughters, lost sheep and coins, wedding banquets and first seats at table, stewards and workers in a vineyard. His people could tell that this man knew them by heart. They saw themselves in the story; therefore, they either hung on his words or they hung him on the Cross. In a less agricultural society, we might choose different images for our stories than shepherds and vineyards. But Jesus remains a model as story-teller. His stories are not just information but invitation—invitation to enter into the story and face ourselves and our God. Like Nathan who tells David the story of the rich man who robbed the poor man, such story-tellers can say to us, "You are the man" (cf. 2 Sam. 12:1-15).

Each of us also has a personal story. In fact, to be a person is to have a story—a narrative which links together in sequence the isolated events of our lives so that we can look at these events in their entirety and discern how our personal identity takes shape in our story. We noted how theologians speak of the Word-event of Jesus; his first message to us, his word-deed, is his life of healing, forgiveness, reconciliation, rooted in his Father's love which brings life out of death.

Each of us proclaims a word-deed, of healing or of wounding. Each of us has a personal story and identity which we proclaim to those who know us. We may choose to talk about our story and share our faith about how we are moving through this pilgrimage of death to life. Even if we do not talk about our story, people will still hear our word-deed. Our lives speak louder than our words. If our word-deed is one of healing and resurrected life, people might hear in it the Word of the Lord.

The point of all this is to broaden ministries of the Word beyond just preaching and teaching. Stories of faith and word-deeds are constantly shared between friend and friend, parents and children, lover and beloved. People with or without master's degrees in religious education who know God and themselves by heart are perhaps the more ordinary and effective ministers of the Word.

Prophets

Prophets do not bring revelations so much as they awaken others to the presence of God and the revelation that has already happened and is happening in their own lives. Prophets do not predict the future; they are so in touch with the present that they can discern the shape of the future based upon the evils or the promises of the present. Prophets know the signs of the time by heart.

I want to single out just one aspect of prophets as ministers of the Word: because prophets know the signs of the times, they can discern our identity as a people through our cultural story. There are not only personal stories; each people and nation has a cultural story, a narrative which gives pattern and purpose to its identity as a people. For example, in *The Broken Covenant* Robert Bellah identifies the American story as a story of a people convinced they were chosen by God to build a Promised Land in which God's covenant of freedom would extend to all the oppressed. That story gives pattern and purpose to so many events in American history. But Bellah also functions as a prophet in touch with our times. He speaks of a *broken* covenant and a present time of trial when new crises test our ability to extend that covenant to the most oppressed at home and the Third World abroad.

Prophets have forever ministered God's Word by raising our consciousness to look at our people's story and by challenging our social conscience to include within the covenant all those whom God would include.

Educators

Already we have seen how God is the great image-maker who images himself not only in Jesus but in the world and in people. We proclaimed the principle: we cannot get closer to God than through his images. Educators invite us to draw close to the images; I do not mean only religious educators.

Educators of small children who work with those little bundles of protoplasm during the critical years and help develop their potential for appreciating images deserve our special reverence. Those early years are the time when we develop our nerve ends, our senses, our antennae for the world. Too often those nerve ends are crushed and the antennae shoved in. George Leonard, in *Education and Ecstacy*, tells of his daughter who was alive to her senses and loved to fill up butcher paper with pictures before she started school. By the time she reached fourth grade, her creativity had been effectively crushed. She was taught to draw only between lines and that skies are always blue and that people always have just two legs. Leonard tried some therapy. He took her to a sound and light show and bombarded her with color, imagery, and music. All she could say was, "Wow!" Out came the butcher paper and the creativity began flowing again.

Not all children are lucky enough to receive such therapy. The following is a poem from an anonymous seventeen year old, entitled "About School":

> He always wanted to say things. But no one understood.
> He always wanted to explain things. But no one cared.
> So he drew.
> Sometimes he would just draw and it wasn't anything. He
> wanted to carve it in stone or write it in the sky.
> He would lie out on the grass and look up in the sky and it
> would be only him and the sky and the things inside, that
> needed saying.
> And it was after that, that he drew the picture. It was a
> beautiful picture. He kept it under the pillow and would
> let no one see it.
> And he would look at it every night and think about it. And
> when it was dark, and his eyes were closed, he could still
> see it.
> When he started school he brought it with him. Not to show
> anyone, but just to have with him like a friend.

It was funny about school.

He sat in a square, brown desk like all the other square, brown desks and he thought it should be red.

And his room was square, brown, like the other rooms. And it was tight and close. And stiff.

He hated to hold the pencil and the chalk, with his arm stiff and his feet flat on the floor, stiff, and with the teacher watching and watching.

And then he had to write numbers. And they weren't anything. They were worse than the letters that could be something if you put them together.

And the numbers were tight and square and he hated the whole thing.

The teacher came and spoke to him. She told him to wear a tie like all the other boys. He said he didn't like them and she said it didn't matter.

After that, they drew. And he drew all yellow and it was the way he felt about morning. And it was beautiful.

The teacher came and smiled at him. "What's this?" she said. "Why don't you draw something like Ken's drawing? Isn't that beautiful?"

It was all questions.

After that his mother bought him a tie, and he always drew airplanes and rocket shops like everyone else.

And he threw the old picture away.

And when he lay out alone looking at the sky, it was big and blue and all of everyting—but he wasn't anymore.

He was square inside and brown, and his hands were stiff, and he was like anyone else.

And the thing inside him that needed saying didn't need saying anymore.

It had stopped pushing. It was crushed. Stiff.

Like everything else.

One week after writing those lines, that young man committed suicide.

There are many other walking dead who still live but whose images from inside never push and whose senses are numb to images from outside. To that extent, God in his images has died.

Thank God there are educators who summon us to life! One

marvelous example is Sylvia Ashton-Warner, teacher of pre-school aborigine children in New Zealand. She teaches reading through experiences and images. For example, she asks, "What happened at home today?" The child may answer, "Father was hugging Mother." Sylvia responds, "Would you like to know the word for that? It's spelled L-O-V-E. That's your word for today. Let's put it on a piece of cardboard, hang it round your neck. Now, go tell everyone about your word and what it means." How far this is from "Dick and Jane" and "See Dick run!" Knowing words charged with such experiences of love, perhaps those children will one day discover the God of love present in their lives.

The process continues in later years when educators in physical sciences invite learners into the mysteries of the universe; and gurus of history, the social sciences, literature and language arts invite them to enter the mystery of persons and of themselves. In their classrooms, these educators normally will not raise issues of explicit religious faith. At other times, in the context of prayer or religious education, each person will discern whether or not he/she interprets these images as sacred places of God's presence. But if educators do not explore the images with us, we have little to interpret.

This presumes a humanistic view of education which goes beyond the factual information level to the appreciation level of meaning and value for human life. This means the historian Dilthey's approach to his discipline—what is the meaning of these events in human terms? It means Peter Berger's approach to sociology. He says the ideal sociologist is intensively, endlessly, shamelessly interested in the doings of humans. It means psychologist Abraham Maslow's approach to all education. He claims the trouble with much of American education is that it does not raise ultimate questions, value questions that make a difference in the lives of people. As a footnote, I might add that even theology has not been devoid of speculation that has little to do with human life. Therefore, we need more of what Karl Rahner calls "theological anthropology"—talk of God (*theos*) ultimately should have something to do with talk of man (*anthropos*).

If educators raise ultimate questions of value and meaning, then the ground has been tilled for faith. Enter religious educators, strictly speaking. In terms of what has been said, the religious educator is, first, an educator—with immense respect for the person, with skills to "lead forth" (Latin: *ex ducere*) the personal stories and images of people so they can be put in dialogue with the human family and the world. Second, they are religious—persons, themselves on the pilgrimage of faith, who know also the images and stories of fellow believers, especially Jesus. Then the dialogue may be between the stories of our contemporaries and the stories of our fellow travelers of our Christian community of faith, past and present. In that dialogue, persons can raise the ultimate questions of value and meaning arising from sharing their stories and discern that they are not the answers to their own questions. The Good News is that their questions can lead to God.

Preachers

A "preacher's tone" is usually a good sign that the preacher does not know the Christian story "by heart." He speaks with the imperious and distant tones of an observer rather than with the empathy of a fellow pilgrim in the human drama.

Preachers should be master story-tellers. Those chosen by the Christian community to officially proclaim the Word of God should be master listeners to all the stories of people in whom that Word has taken flesh: the stories in Scripture, in the history of God's people, in great literature in which great authors image the human adventure, in their own lives and the lives of their people living today. Especially at Eucharist, their task is to put all these stories into dialogue with Jesus' story. In some way, all human stories are stories about how each of us dies and rises. At the Eucharist, therefore, the preacher does not merely inform but, like Jesus, he invites people to see their dying and rising in relationship to the dying and rising of Jesus. He invites them to let Jesus travel with them on their exodus to the Father, and he invites them to give thanks to a God who saves their story from dead ends and offers resurrection.

Too often preachers use the right-handed language of theology and the classroom rather than the left-handed language of story and the heart. Preachers need to know theology, because theology equips them to analyze stories of past and present and discern their common meanings. But when they enter the pulpit, they should become more story-teller and poet than theologian.

Poets

A pioneer English catechist, Canon Drinkwater, once distinguished four kinds of language in religious education: scientific difficult (Thomas Aquinas), scientific simple (Baltimore catechism), poetic difficult (Shakespeare), poetic simple (the parables of Jesus). He insisted that the language of most religious education should be poetic simple.

Jesus was a poet in the sense that, like all poets, he was deeply in touch with his primary experiences, with his own identity and story, with what the poet Gerard Manley Hopkins calls "the dearest freshness deep-down things." Like all poets, Jesus found the words and stories to which we can respond, "Aha! That's what I knew but couldn't say. That's what I've been experiencing. That's what I knew but didn't know that I knew."

Karl Rahner says that we don't have to be poets to be Christians. He also says that great Christianity and great poetry go together, because the poet is one who has radically faced who he/she is. In that sense, there needs to be a bit of the poet in all ministers of the Word. After all, the most compelling ministers of God's Word are those who know themselves, their people, and their God by heart.

Priests

Rahner also asserts, however, that priests should be poets. In terms of this chapter, priests should be those chosen by the community and from the community as the masters of imagination and left-handed thinking—the master story-tellers, preachers, educators who "lead forth" our images, and poets who have faced radically who they are and who we are.

As an aside, I have to admit that this job description of the priest runs contrary to much of our past seminary training which screened out strange people like poets and trained men with a vengeance in right-handed thinking. It also avoids the fact that a priestly people in most cases has little to say as yet in the determination of the master poets among them who will be ordained to the specialized ministry of priesthood. It does suggest that if left-handed thinking, poetry, and creation of stories and parables are desirable qualities in the priest (since they are qualities in Jesus), women in our culture would be important persons to look to to find those who resemble Christ.

I am distinguishing here between priest and pastor. We shall look at the ministry of pastor in terms of community-building and suggest that, although pastors today are almost always priests, that need not be the case. In fact, many of the skills of pastors are right-handed—skills of organization, administration, facilitating groups—and it may be too much to expect those skills in all left-handed priests. In fact, it may be dangerous. We are looking today for pastors who are able to set up, guide, and support such structures as parish councils; we are looking for managerial skills. Such managers may also be poets, but it may be too much to expect both in one person.

Not only in Christianity but in all religions, the priest is primarily regarded as the holy man. In every survey I have seen recently about people's expectations of priests, top on the list were such qualities as: a man of God, a holy man, a spiritual leader, a man of prayer. That is akin not to the manager but to what religions often call the "mystagogue"—one who has entered the mysteries, who invites us into the mysteries, who has tasted the Lord, traveled with him through the mysteries of death and life, pain and ecstasy; in other words, the one who knows the Lord, himself, and us by heart. He also, like Jesus, is the one who in prayer and celebration is the poet who can find words to reveal mystery, not in the language of analysis but in the patterns and rhythms of story and gesture and movement and ritual. He is more like the shaman of primitive tribes than the executive of a large corporation.

Finally, the priest is more image and symbol of God and Church than he is definition. Holy Orders is a sacrament, meaning not just the rite, but the people who enter the order of priests. They are chosen because we find in them symbols and sacraments of what we all should be—persons who know by heart.

Conversation Starters

1) What did your religious education help you learn "by heart"?

2) Did your faith in God help you through the most painful time in your life?

3) Did your faith in God help you rejoice at the most happy time in your life?

4) What do you do most naturally, left-handed or right-handed thinking?

5) What is your favorite novel?

6) Can you name anyone who, in your opinion, is a prophet today?

7) Did you find school "square and brown and stiff"?

8) Who are your teachers now?

9) If you were "preacher for a day," what gospel story would you choose and what other stories would you tell to relate the gospel to life?

10) Do you read poetry?

11) What do you look for most in a priest?

12) How should candidates for priesthood be chosen, trained, and recommended for ordination?

13) How do you feel about women priests?

Where I Stand

1) My knowledge of God and Jesus is . . .

2) The most important question for me about my life right now is . . .

3) When it comes to expressing my feelings, I usually . . .

4) The person in the gospels most like me is . . .

5) I feel our nation is . . .

6) My favorite teacher was . . .

7) The best homily I ever heard was . . .

8) My favorite poem is . . .

9) The priest who has most touched my life is . . .

5 Ministries of Building Community

Where I Stand

1) I feel my neighborhood is . . .

2) Conversation with my friends is . . .

3) The three persons who most share my values and way of looking at life are . . .

4) When I'm in a large gathering of people, I feel . . .

5) If I celebrate the sacrament of reconciliation face to face, I feel . . .

6) I feel my work is . . .

7) I believe marriage today is . . .

8) I believe families today are . . .

> The customary experiences and ways of perceiving which in the past led to belief in God have been altered, or have lost their direct and spontaneous power. Many men, consequently, no longer have access to God. They are, simply, unaware of God. Their unawareness does not mean that God does not exist; *only that he does not exist effectively for them.* [Michael Novak, "The Unawareness of God," *The God Experience*, ed. Joseph P. Whelan. New York: Newman Press, 1971, p. 7.]

Novak goes on to claim that one such experience presently altered in or absent altogether from American life is the experience of community. He depicts American life as a great cocktail party where individuals wander about behind their masks, making small talk, talking past each other, drugged by drink rather than intoxicated by geniune friendship and community. He also sees Americans as the Lone Ranger, the Marlboro man, the loner who sings with the Beatles, "All the lonely people!" (who include "Father McKenzie"). Since God is Community and since God is Trinity, Novak claims that lives empty of trinity and community are lives empty of that which is most like God.

Novak's remarks may find some resonance in our own experiences of emptiness, especially if we number ourselves among "the lonely crowd." However, his vision of community seems limited largely to a behavioral science image of intimate groups who share feelings and friendship, with show-and-tell sensitivity sessions at home, in close neighborhoods, or marathons with psychotherapists. That vision may capture the rapture of Big Sur but fails to unveil the ecstasy of Mt. Sinai where God offers covenant and community.

Community (*koinonia*) is a word often used with little sense of precise meaning. Before we discuss ministries which build community, we need some sense of what it is that is to be built. Therefore, we shall first look at community from various perspectives—biblical, theological, sociological, and psychological. Second, we shall look at various ministries which build community, with an attempt to move beyond a narrow view which would limit those ministries to priests or community organizers.

A Biblical Perspective

In the experience of Jews and Christians, God is the great community organizer. The communities of the Old and the New Covenant do not arise from encounter sessions, sensitivity sessions, or coffee klatches. They arise from God's choice, God's free and loving initiative reaching out to his people, calling them to himself, uniting them to each other.

Nothing else could explain Israel's origin as God's People. "If Yahweh set his heart on you and chose you, it was not because you outnumbered other peoples; you were the least of all peoples. It was for love of you and to keep the oath he swore to your fathers that Yahweh brought you out with his mighty hand and redeemed you from the house of slavery, from the power of Pharaoh king of Egypt" (Deut. 7:7-8).

Nothing else explains Christians' origins as God's People. "Before the world was made, [God the Father] chose us, chose us in Christ, to be holy and spotless, and to live through love in his presence, determining that we should become his adopted sons, through Jesus Christ for his own kind purposes, to make us praise the glory of his grace, his free gift to us in the Beloved, in whom, through his blood, we gain our freedom, the forgiveness of our sins" (Eph. 1:4-7).

With Novak, I shall affirm later that God calls us as a community so that in our lives together we might image his love and experience his presence through each other. However, this biblical perspective on covenant-community reveals at least two dimensions of community which go beyond that of human friendship and intimacy.

First, we affirmed earlier that, for the believer, only God can make a man. For the believer, only God can build real community. That which binds us together is God's life of love. God the Father has raised Jesus in his humanity to live that life forever, and already he has raised us with him. He has graced us with the gifts which make us a community—poverty of spirit, gentleness, hunger and thirst for justice, mercy, purity in heart, peacemaking (cf. Matt. 5:3-10). Our faith is that people do not live this astonishing life of self-giving love, made flesh especially in Jesus, unless God gives us such power. Our faith, also, is that our ministries of building community are not self-initiated. They are ultimately a sharing of gifts which are initiated and brought to birth in us by God.

Second, although we hope that most people will know the Father through experiences of care and love in community, especially with family and friends, the believer affirms that, even when such communities escape us, we still live in communion with God who offers his love. We follow a man scorned by most communities in his own time. "Jerusalem, Jerusalem, . . . How often have I longed to gather your children, as a hen gathers her brood under her wings, and you refused!" (Luke 13:34). We hope most people will discover the God of love through people who live in love. That is the normal way. But, like Jesus, we may discover the God of love and compassion precisely when people leave us abandoned and yearning for love. With him, perhaps we can only murmur, "Father, into your hands I commit my spirit" (Luke 23:46). With Augustine, we cry, "Our hearts are restless until they rest in Thee."

A Theological Perspective

Of all the possible theological reflections gleaned from reflection upon the biblical experience, I offer four which are especially important for ministers who build community.

First, community is the goal of Christianity. God is building a communion of saints, a lasting city. Augustine describes heaven as "one Christ, loving Himself." Jesus prays, "Father, may they be one in us, as you are in me and I am in you" (John 17:21). Sin is all that which shatters this oneness: the rugged individualism of selfishness, greed, envy, violence, prejudice, injustice. Salvation is precisely that which brings at-one-ment: self-giving love, gentleness, thirst for justice, mercy, peacemaking. For that kind of community are we made.

Second, when theologians call the Church a sacrament, they affirm that this community is called to be a "visible sign of all these invisible graces," a sign lifted among the nations, salt of the earth and light to the world showing what life can be when people accept God's at-one-ment. "See how those Christians love one another," the Romans used to say. Christians, with a knowing smile, could then respond, "See also how *God* loves us, because those who live in love, live in God and God in them" (cf. 1 John 4:7-21). The Church is more than friendship groups and human love; but when Christians live in friendship and love, they live out their vocation as sacraments—visible signs of the God who is more than they themselves. Building community, therefore, is heart and center of our vocation as Church.

Third, community for a covenant-people chosen by God is also more than friendship groups in the sense that we are a people with a mission and vocation grounded not just on our choice of each other but on God's choice of us. People sometimes claim that huge parishes are more mobs than communities, because people don't know each other. That is partly true, but vast throngs of people aren't the only issue. The issue is also faith. If that throng really believed that God loves us and showers his gifts upon us, if they really believed that we are a people on a mission to share that Good News, they would be drawn together in a community of vision and mission like the crowd in John's vision of heaven: "Then I saw before me a huge crowd which no one could count. . . . They cried out in a loud voice, 'Salvation is from our God. . . .'" (Rev. 7:9, 10). If we are a people who share the faith that "salvation is from our God," if we share values, purpose, a sense of direction that we are a people with a mission which is going somewhere, if we have the Good News of salvation to share, if like Jesus we have the reign of the Father as our goal and hope, we shall experience a community of vision and purpose. If we truly believe we are a pilgrim people on exodus through death to life, then we are a people with cause to celebrate when we gather, no matter how large our number. When we gather at Eucharist, we shall lift the rafters with our songs of joy. When we leave Eucharist, we shall lift up our sisters and brothers by sharing Good News.

Fourth, having said all that, I must still assert with much regret that many parishes have not given their rafters a lift for a good long time. I have to admit that, although large groups can share value and purpose which ground community, usually shared purpose and mission are built in smaller communities. Certainly, that is what such movements as Marriage Encounter, Cursillo, and charismatic prayer groups are saying to the wider Church. Might they offer some direction for the parish?

That is a theological, not just a tactical question. To move from a vision of Church which still calls an immense number of people a "parish family" to a vision of Church which sees the parish as a gathering of smaller communities and families is to shift images of Church.

A clarion call to shift, or at least expand, our images of Church came from Bishop Albert Ottenweller at the 1975 meeting of American bishops. Speaking as a pastor, Bishop Ottenweller proclaimed the now-famous "funnel theory" which has since become a clerical household word. He spoke of the pastor who felt like he had a funnel over his head, and down the funnel came all the projects and programs concocted since Vatican II. They landed right on top of his head. The catch is that the parish, as it is now structured, most often cannot get those programs off its head and into the lives of people.

Bishop Ottenweller suggested that most parishes are structured as institutions, not communities. He described institutions as large service centers to which people with all sorts of needs come. Many of those needs are personal needs, and many of the offerings since Vatican II offer more personal care—a more personal experience of reconciliation in the revised sacrament of reconciliation, more personal initiation into the Church in the new Rite of Christian Initiation for Adults, more personal preparation for the sacraments in families, more personal prayer and spiritual direction in prayer groups. Professionals at a service center cannot and should not handle all that.

What is needed, then, is an image of the parish which sees it not as one large service center but many communities within the larger group.

People in those smaller groups offer their gifts and make known their needs. The bishop suggested that a parish of 1500 families would require 400 well-trained lay ministers to service those needs in smaller communities of faith. This does not mean they need the skills of full-time professional ministers; the training does not necessarily mean a degree in theology, for example. It might mean releasing gifts they have but don't know they have—for example, a good ear for listening and a lively faith for praying. The theological vision of parish behind such efforts, however, would be one which might finally cut through a "we-they" understanding of Church which sees "we," the parishioners, ministered to only by "they," the professional ministers. We would move to build community not through "they," the Church who ministers *to* us, but "we," the Church, who minister *with* one another.

Perspectives from Sociology and Psychology

I shall conclude with two thoughts from the world of sociological surveys and one from the psychological couch.

Sociologist Robert Nisbet uses two German words to distinguish between two types of community: *Gemeinschaft* and *Gesellschaft*. *Gemeinschaft* communities, described in Nisbet's book, *The Social Bond*, are those for which Michael Novak yearns. They are those which encompass our full personalities and not just single aspects of our lives. Essential is the quality of strong cohesion to one another, as in tightly-knit families, village communities, friendship groups, perhaps ethnic groups. *Gesellschaft* communities, on the other hand, may be large or small, but what is crucial is that they engage persons in only one or a few aspects of their total life. They are commonly founded around a few specific interests or purposes, and would include relationships at work, at a social club, or in a political organization.

In *Unsecular Man*, Andrew Greeley disputes the claim of Novak that we live in a more impersonal society—dehumanized and devoid of *Gemeinschaft* communities. He says the number of *Gemeinschaft* relationships probably has not declined since our peasant grandparents left their villages in Europe; and he claims that it is quite possible that the quality of these relationships has improved, e.g., intimacy between husbands and wives today. He says the difference may be, rather, that larger blocks of our time must be spent in a world of *Gesellschaft* relationships at work, or on the freeway on the way to work, in an achievement-oriented society. In such a world, people may long for more and for deeper *Gemeinschaft* communities.

In such a world, Christian community-builders who do not limit the experience of God to *Gemeinschaft* relationships can still agree that the God of love is often most deeply present through such relationships. They may hear a special call to strengthen bonds in marriage, family, the neighborhood, or the parish. Among religious communities, those which seem to flourish today are those which offer more personal community experiences, e.g., parishes which have divided the total population into smaller block or neighborhood groups.

Second, sociologists also assert, once again with a German accent, that even *Gemeinschaft* communities do not survive long on superficial feelings of intimacy. They demand a shared *Weltanschauung*, a shared outlook with common values. This recalls earlier comments about building community by helping people clarify their sense of mission, purpose, direction, and the values they cherish. To the beat of what distant drummer are we marching? For believers, perhaps in a simple age, the cadence beat out by the local pastor or authority figure would keep us in step and in line. In a more complex world in which all sorts of values and worldviews compete for our attention, sociologist Peter Berger notes there is no longer one "sacred canopy" of Christianity under which most people gather. There is a vast array of "sacred umbrellas," ranging from the Moonies, through the mainline religions, to secular humanism. Community-builders will need to help people personalize their religion by consciously choosing their heritage and the values covered by one of the many umbrellas carried in the parade. Assaulted by the cacophony of so many conflicting worldviews, believers personally need to make the rhythms of Jesus their own if the community of his followers hopes to stay in tune.

Finally, from psychology comes the perspective that, although there may be tension between affirming the rights of persons and also preserving the rights of the entire community, the healthiest communities are those in which the rights, differences and gifts of persons are respected. The healthiest persons are those who enjoy and contribute to the life of the community.

We have heard the humanistic psychologists assert that the goal of personhood is community: communion with self (all the dynamisms within us, e.g., our unconscious, our feelings, our dreams and memories, our bodies, our conscious life), communion with the world, communion with other people. Each of us has a personal center which is uniquely our own: our unique gifts and weaknesses, our history, our values, our basic attitudes toward life. But that personal center is achieved through our relationships with others, through the ways they affirm us, challenge us, confront us, accept us, call forth our gifts. Psychologist Erik Erickson, for example, affirms that the identity crisis of adolescence is resolved through the intimacy and choice of vocation during young adulthood, and that the continued growth of people at mid-life comes when they generate life for others. Community-builders, therefore, who offer communion through intimacy and service and generativity are also person-builders.

Having affirmed God as the primary community-builder, and having clarified just what it is we are helping to build, we can now identify four of the many ministries of community building: lovers, parents, pastors, parish councils.

Lovers

In the jargon of the sociologists, lovers are the "significant others" who build persons through communion. Lovers are the great builders of *Gemeinschaft* communities of intimacy and friendship.

Earlier I described love as "letting-be": letting other persons be all that they can uniquely be. Lovers lose themselves in the beloved. While they are lost "in there," they discover the beauty and creativity and the many-splendored things waiting to be released. Lovers help their beloved discover gifts they never knew they had. Eunice Shriver once talked of her young, fearful, rigid brother, Bob Kennedy. Under Ethel's care, she said, "How he blossomed!"

A lover's or a friend's honest criticism can also reveal our self-deception, our dishonesty and laziness, and so help us become more authentically what we are called to become. That honesty often demands an even greater loss of self for the sake of the beloved: a loss of fear, of security, of strong walls of defense which guard us from taking risks which might mean rejection.

A special ministry of lovers can be their care for other couples in love. In many parishes couples are gathering with other couples to help them prepare for marriage or enrich their marriage. They share their experience of how they communicate, how they respect each other's freedom and individuality, how they share their visions and make decisions together, how they take care of children and budgets, dishes and diapers, what their sexuality means to them, what their differences mean to them.

Parents

Parents are two lovers whose community allows a third person to be. These lovers do for children what they do for each other. They are the builders of family, that *Gemeinschaft* community in which most of us first discover our gifts, who we want to be, what we cherish and hold dear. Parents, then, are creators not just of protoplasm but of persons —persons who become themselves in and through their relationships.

In and through relationships to parents, children most often develop their relationship to God and their understanding of how God builds community. Through parents who take the first step in forgiveness, they learn of the biblical God who takes the initiative in loving his people. Through parents who are faithful and stick with children even when they are "terrible two's" and even more "terrible teens," children will experience the fidelity of Yahweh who never leaves his people. Through masculine and feminine ways of loving, both present in each male and female parent, children experience the many ways that God the Father gives power and strength and God the Mother offers mercy and tenderness. Through the love of parents, children learn we are made for the God who is love. Through the ways families hurt and wound each other, children learn their theology of sin which is anything that shatters unity and love. Through family community, children first experience God who is community.

We have also seen that communities are built through shared values and a shared worldview. It is common parlance today to speak of parents as the primary educators. I know some parents who resent that and see it as a way for teachers to escape their responsibilities and disclaim their failure. In religious education, parents usually will not be the primary teachers of doctrine. At least during the early years, they will be the primary communicators of values, whether they know it or not. Values are more caught than taught, and parents, through the way they live and love, are always pitching values. So many young people today seem rootless and have difficulty deciding their vocation or making any decision. We desperately need the ministry of parents who build communities of shared values upon which young people can make decisions, communities which encourage young people to listen for the beat of a distant drummer which calls them to commitment.

Pastors

I conclude with two more church-related ministries—pastors and parish councils.

Note that I say pastor, not priest. In almost every case today, say one and you say the other. We have already seen, however, that the priest who is a poet and story-teller cannot ordinarily be expected also to be a community-organizer and administrator. So I speak of pastor with an openness to the possibility that some day many pastors may not be priests. Already, in some dioceses, sisters and permanent deacons are serving as pastors.

The pastor is more needed than ever before precisely because of our deepened understanding of expanded ministries. The pastor has often been the one-man band who did (or tried to do) all the ministries and who sometimes felt burdened because he was expected to have all the gifts. This is the pastor with the funnel over his head into which every project and expectation was poured since Vatican II.

Some now see the pastor as an orchestra leader who helps others discover their gifts, invites them to play their part, and helps them play in harmony. I find that image too neat and tidy. At least, for the moment (and I believe for a long time to come) I sense that the pastor is more like the circus master of a three-ring circus. This is hardly an orchestra in which each player promptly comes in at the drop of a baton. Rather, we have at least three rings going, with all kinds of talents shown and performances given, and just a few clowns.

In the midst of all this, pastors as circus masters need tremendous gifts: the gift of self-confidence so they are not threatened by performances they cannot render and talents they do not have; the gift of listening and discerning which helps other people discover their gifts; the gift of reconciling and peacemaking which heals the wounds of those who fall from the heights; the gift of vision which keeps them in touch with the total picture so that no ring in the circus dominates the show and excludes others with their talents; the gift of organization (not just administration) which helps them plan and facilitate with others the life of all the members; the gift of patience with the clowns and the gift of welcome to those who are still spectators; the gift of celebration when the entire community gathers to rejoice in their gifts and their care for each other. The new word is that the pastor is the great enabler of ministries, the great facilitator, who makes contributions to the community precisely by enabling the community to contribute to each other and to their God.

Parish Councils

In some ways, what is said of the pastor can also be said of parish councils and committees. These should be the vision people who give spiritual leadership. These are the prayer people who discern God's presence in our lives and help others discover his presence. These are the organization people in the best sense of that term—the people in touch with the life of the organism which is the human family, in touch with God's gifts to the community and the hurts and wounds of the community, so that gift can be applied to need.

There is bad news. I lead parish council workshops on many weekends, and to talk to some of those councils in terms of vision people and prayer people is to sound like the circus clown. It is easy to understand why this should be so. A Church which did not always encourage lay people to be visionaries or to tap their gifts of faith is now seeing the results in some people who are only yes men or women to the pastor, who are so angry that they try power plays with the pastor, and who see their roles in terms of decisions about nuts and bolts and not the spirituality and shared values of the parish. I know of one parish council which spent one of its first meetings arguing about the brash young associate pastor who had silenced the beils at the Consecration. Another parish council spent hours coming to a major decision about a dishwasher. Another censured the pastor for painting the flagpole without their permission. I suggested they take a poll among people on the street and also search the gospels to find just how much concern there is among Jesus and people for bells, dishwashers, and flagpoles.

There is also Good News. Some parish councils are praying together. Some are learning skills about how they might discern the needs of people and the gospel's response to those needs. Some are learning how to run a meeting. Ever so slowly, they are becoming the builders of a community which reveals the loving presence of the God of the covenant. To spell out the ministries of the parish council would take many books. I am saying that they have something to do with discerning the needs of people and the gifts of God, something to do with setting broad policies based on the values of the gospel, and very much to do, therefore, with prayer and spiritual leadership in building community.

Conversation Starters

1) Do you believe people today lack deep and close relationships?

2) Was there a time when you felt abandoned by everyone?

3) Have you ever wanted to say, "See how those Christians love each other"?

4) What are three purposes of your parish?

5) Name four kinds of well-trained lay ministers which your parish needs.

6) Name two *Gemeinschaft* and four *Gesellschaft* communities in your life.

7) Have you ever considered changing religions?

8) Has any person discovered a gift in you which you didn't know you had?

9) What are six issues that couples should talk over before marriage?

10) At what time were your parents most faithful to you?

11) What was your mother's greatest gift, and your father's—to yourself? to others?

12) Do you believe all pastors should be priests?

13) Is your pastor a one-man band, an orchestra leader, or a circus-master?

Where I Stand

1) I feel my neighborhood is . . .

2) Conversation with my friends is . . .

3) The three persons who most share my values and way of looking at life are . . .

4) When I'm in a large gathering of people, I feel . . .

5) If I celebrate the sacrament of reconciliation face to face, I feel . . .

6) I feel my work is . . .

7) I believe marriage today is . . .

8) I believe families today are . . .

6 Ministries of Celebrating

Where I Stand

1) If I could relive one week of my life, I would choose . . .

2) The last time I thought seriously of suicide was . . .

3) Four critical turning points in my autobiography are . . .

4) My next important future decision will be about . . .

5) With the person I love most, I still can't seem to be completely united in the area of . . .

6) I believe in God the Father who . . .

7) I believe in Jesus who . . .

8) I believe in the Holy Spirit who . . .

9) The liturgical celebration which touched me most deeply was . . .

In the last scene of Thornton Wilder's play, *Our Town*, Emily, who had recently died, finds she can relive part of her life on earth. She asks to return to her home town to relive those cherished moments, and her wish is granted. Back home in Grover's Corners she finds fond memories. She also sees all that she had missed, and she exclaims:

> ". . . I didn't realize. So all that was going on and we never noticed. . . ." [After bidding her adieu to those people and things which have become part of her, she continues:] "Oh, earth, you're too wonderful for anybody to realize you."

She looks toward the stage manager and asks abruptly,
through her tears:
"Do any human beings ever realize life while they live it?
—every, every minute?"
[The stage manager replies:]
"No." *Pause.* "The saints and poets, maybe—they do some."

Celebrations are there to help us "realize life while we live it
—every, every minute." Celebrations send us deep into the human
moments of birth, reconciliation, married love, communion meal,
sickness, and death to discover the presence of the Lord offering life.
In Sr. José Hobday's terms, they "invest the minute with meaning,
the decade with direction" ("To Serve and Not to Be Served: The
Church as Servant in Our Time," in *Ministering in a Servant Church*,
ed. by Francis A. Eigo, OSA.) They are sacred times set apart so that
we might discern the sacredness of all times.

Ministries of celebrating, however, more than any other ministries, most easily become liturgical. What originated in human lives,
the grateful celebration of God's presence in all of human life, becomes restricted to the sanctuary. God's real presence in all those
moments when he draws us forth from death to life narrows to his Real
Presence in Eucharist and, even then, Eucharist seen not as the action
of communion meal but as distinct objects of bread and wine on the
altar. Official ministries become limited to lectors, acolytes, deacons,
etc., who await us on Sunday in the churches, and fail to include those
who journey daily with us through our human times of death and resurrection and give us cause to offer thanks in the churches.
Therefore, we need to go back to the roots of ritual. We need to
retrace the steps our liturgical forefathers took when they stepped
from daily life to church celebrations, from human experience to religious experience, from human stories to God's story. These steps
include: listening to what is happening in our lives and the lives of
others by sharing our stories with one another; then searching out the
meaning of our life experiences by asking questions of meaning—what
is the meaning of the moment? then discovering whether or not those
questions are answered by ourselves or through communion with
others, and whether or not those others include *the* Other whom we
call Father; and finally, celebrating our thanksgiving if we discover
God's presence in those times of death and resurrection. As a footnote,

I might mention that this process of moving through human experience to the discernment of God's presence in our story is the same process which calls new Christians to initiation and conversion through catechesis and liturgical celebration in the new *Rite of Christian Initiation for Adults.*

Stories

First, we share stories of death.

> A woman about her marriage: "One of the things I'd never have dreamed possible is the way a man and woman who married for love can within eight years become a brother and sister—respect and even a kind of love, but not an iota of anything else."

> A policeman angered by the language of some college students and frustrated by his job: "I went to confession later and told the priest I'd sworn back at them. . . . He said he wanted me to know that he was behind us in what we, the police, are trying to do. I said, 'Father, if you know what we're trying to do, I wish you'd let me know, and that would be two of us that know.' I didn't hear a sound out of him."

> A 19-year-old, already worn out by her inability to change the world: "Our parents hate us, our politicians desert us, our hopes simply grow old and die. I sound as though I am wallowing in self-pity because the world is too harsh. I'm not. I'm only very tired."

We hope we can also share stories of death-resurrection.

> A woman about her marriage: "We've been married for over twenty years, and the most enjoyable thing either of us does—that is, outside of the intimate things—is to sit and talk by the hour. The big part of our lives is completely mutual."

> A student on friendship: "For too many years I've tried to go it alone, after my father died. I was hurt, and I selfishly

enjoyed it. A few weeks ago I let a person into my life—my first friendship in five years. And for the first time in five years, I'm letting myself feel again."

A man about his attempted suicide: "I looked at my life and said, 'No!' Then, in a whirlwind I experienced nothingness and the abyss, the void beyond death, and the empty. Crying, I searched—found death, experienced it, and began the long return to preparation, for life is preparation, preparation for death. For in my death was a cry—lonely, frightening, horrifying, and yet a Terrible Reply. With that reply lay the realization that I was not alone. I was in something, a part of something greater than myself. Something that said yes to life and yes to me, and I began to crawl back into life aware of a mystery that was both me yet beyond me, and slowly I became less mystery to myself. I was learning to love, and mystery took on a name and mystery's name was Presence. Mystery became Presence through others in my life."

First, then, the stories. A marriage flounders. A child dies. A job runs out of gas and stops. An old man smiles us back to life. A son comes home. A friend forces open our shell. The system smothers us. A loved one wakes us with a kiss. Note that the story can be one of human pain or joy, depravity or grandeur. No matter, as long as it moves us beyond looking at just the time of day to discern the meaning of minutes and the direction of decades which proclaim whether we shall live or die.

Questions

Then, the questions. Where have I come from? Where am I going? Why is there so much evil in me? Why is there so much evil in others? Why am I so blessed? Why are others so good? What did I do to deserve this pain? What did I do to merit this gift? What is a good man, a good woman, a good community? What should I be loyal to? What should I be ready to die for? "What's it all about, Alfie?"

After telling our stories, this second step leads us to search for their meaning, to explore the meaning of our lives. Among others, theologian Karl Rahner suggests that what makes humans differ from beasts is our compulsion to ask questions, to find the human significance in events, even those which seem absurd. These are not the superficial questions of small talk about a world wrung flat, in which Michael Novak claims our deepest experiences are often like a "burp after lunch." This is serious talk about stories in which we are entrapped or liberated, when we crash into our limits and fall back, when our emptiness suddenly seems brimming over with fullness, when we are overwhelmed by death and yet sense the traces of resurrection. These are the climactic events like the Cross which caused Jesus to raise his own ultimate question, "My God, my God, why have you abandoned me?"

Communion with Others

Yet Jesus' final words were, "Into your hands I commit my spirit." No one can say those words for us. In that private place where each of us stands alone, rummaging through the ruins of shattered dreams or gasping in awe at unexpected gifts, we can cringe in self-pity or swagger with self-righteousness. We can turn in to ourselves. Or we can open up like Jesus to others and commit ourselves into their hands, grasping for healing, mercy, and strength or rejoicing in gratitude, praise, and thanksgiving.

If we decide we are not the answers to our own questions, if we turn from the masochism of self-pity and the arrogance of self-made men and women, if we decide that the meaning of our lives cannot be chiseled out by protesting with Simon and Garfunkel "I am a rock, I am an island," then we take a further step toward celebration. Each of us makes a choice that only we can make: that we are not the source of our own healing if we are in pain, that we are not the source of our own gifts if we are in joy. We open ourselves to communion with others who are the source of healing and gift. Like the man cited above who turned from suicide, we hear an affirmation of our life in the mystery of both pain and joy; and mystery becomes Presence in Communion.

That man also said, "Mystery became Presence through others in my life." Our choice of those others determines the scope and place of our celebration. Marxists agree that "no man is an island." For them, the meaning of our lives and our consummate utopia will be found only in communion; but the community remains limited to the human—the kingdom of the proletariat and ultimately the classless society. Therefore, their celebrations will be in plazas festooned with the visages of their leaders.

Again, most psychologists agree that the meaning of persons is discovered only in relationships, in dialogue, in communion with others. For some, however, communion with others does not mean Communion with the Other. Grace can remain "the congruence, empathy, and unconditional postive regard" offered by the patient-centered therapist. Community means only the human communion offered in encounter, marathon, and sensitivity sessions, and there they hold their celebrations.

Some non-believers, who share the care and compassion of believers for the human family, confirm the conviction that life finds meaning only in lives laid down for and with the brothers and sisters. Yet sometimes they are appalled by the enormous greed and lack of caring shown in lives of so-called believers in a communion with God which apparently excludes any communion with humans. They conclude that one cannot believe in heaven and still believe in earth (Albert Camus), and one cannot believe in God and still believe in man (Friedrich Nietzsche). They seek no more than a human community of compassion, and their celebrations are wherever humans heal and caress and empower each other with new life. It is into human hands that they commit their spirits.

Communion with God

There are others who find no human hands which can hold their spirit. With Augustine, their "hearts are restless until they rest in Thee." They do not reject human community. Far from it. They believe it is precisely in human care and compassion that they discover traces and hints of a care more than human. Christians discover those traces especially in the humanity of Jesus: "He who sees me sees the Father" (John 14:9). But believers remain restless. They experience that no human healing and no human gift binds up all the wounds or exhausts our potential for love. In human community they discover possibilities for communion with something more, someone more, a more encompassing Presence, a more enveloping whole, a richer communion with a God they name Allah or Yahweh or Father.

That response is called faith. Faith is not merely acceptance of truths but the surrender of our entire life to God in response to his healing touch and his gift of life. Faith is our basic attitude and stance, coming before creeds and rituals, that in the midst of both pain and joy a Presence reaches out to us summoning us through death to resurrection. That Presence is not proved, but it is also not wishful thinking nor absurd. We do have traces and hints that there is a Presence offering healing and love which is more than human. That Presence also is not captured; there are only hints and traces, most often discovered in human community. But our faith-response is that our praise and thanksgiving is not just fellowship with the crowd but worship of the Father. Faith makes possible religious celebration.

Celebration

Our discovery—that the meaning of our stories resides not in splendid isolation but in our communion with others and with the Other who offer us healing and hope—bursts forth in celebration, in thanksgiving, in Eucharist. For Christians, this discovery should be the origin of sacramental celebrations—not a law which demands that we shall celebrate and give thanks and rejoice "under pain of mortal sin," but our faith not just that "God is" but that "God is for us." Life is for us —healing and hope are not pipe dreams. Essential to every Christian sacrament is our faith that the human stories about the most important moments in our stories (birth, belonging, reconciliation, giving witness, communion meals, marriage, sickness, and death) are also God's story. Our faith is that God is partner to the human adventure and life is his gift. Belonging, reconciliation, love, healing, and resurrection are his gifts. Therefore, with Augustine, "We are Easter Christians, and Alleluia is our song!" Our celebrations give alleluias of faith. Sacramental celebrations, no matter how beautiful the choir or groovy the guitars, are "full of sound and fury, signifying nothing" if there is no faith. The path of sacramental preparation, therefore, is not so much one of choosing Latin or English, baroque music or folk, extended tongues or hands. The basic choice concerns the meaning of our stories, a choice of despair or hope, emptiness or fullness, bitterness or reconciliation, fists clenched in anger or opened in praise and thanksgiving, defiant isolation or grateful communion.

By definition, therefore, authentic Christian celebrations are celebrations of *faith*. They are also celebrations in *community*, not just communion with God but communion with God experienced through communion with others. As for that young man who contemplated suicide, in genuine Christian celebration "Mystery becomes Presence through others in my life," especially Jesus. God has chosen people as the most dynamic sacraments of his Real Presence to us. Vatican II's *Constitution on the Liturgy* affirms Christ's Presence not only in the meal of bread and wine but also in his Word, in the ministers, and in the community gathered in his name (cf. no. 7). The stubborn resistance by some to the communal exchange of peace at Eucharist is perhaps our clearest signal of our failure to proclaim that we cannot swallow the host without swallowing our brother and sister. More positively, our celebrations need to express in ritual what we experience to be true in the rest of our lives: God initiates us to himself through our belonging to a community; God reconciles us to himself through reconciliation to a community; God weds himself to us through marriage to each other; God heals especially through loving family and friends gathered round our sickbed, and God enters into communion with us through our communion with each other. In a sense, God can touch our lives when we are alone in the desert. In celebrations, however, he touches our lives to the extent that we enter into a faith-filled community.

That brings us back where we began: reflection on ministries of celebration. From what has been said, it should be clear that members of this faith-filled community minister to us long before we arrive at church to celebrate. Ministers of the Word will help us tell our stories, and they share with us the stories of our people, especially Jesus' story. Ministers of community-building will help us find the meaning of our stories in communion, reconciliation, and healing so that we have something to celebrate. Ministers of service-healing will be with us, as God is with us on the cross, reaching out to us especially in our pain so that we do not die alone. Ministers of celebrating will help us rejoice and give thanks in countless ways before we arrive at church, just as Jesus did by having supper with Zaccheus and throwing parties for prodigal sons.

What, then, should be the qualities of those who celebrate within the sanctuary? Like liturgy itself, these personal qualities exist in tension—between death and resurrection, the past and the future, listening and speaking.

People Who Know Both Death and Life
The extremes are those who insist, "Beneath every cloud is a silver lining," and those who retort, "Above every silver lining is a cloud!"

The extremes are believers in a sugar daddy deity of peace, love, and joy and people like the priest who once thanked Groucho Marx for bringing such joy into the world. Groucho responded, "And I want to thank you, Father, for taking so much joy out of it."

The roots of our celebrations are in moments of both death and resurrection, pain and joy. If anything, perhaps that word "celebration" speaks too softly of dying. In all those times in our lives when we search for meaning, there is death: a sense of loss, failure, loneliness, of being wrenched from our past. Even in the most joyful times of love, we discover we need to die to self, die to our rugged independence, die to our own needs, and surrender to another. Good ministers of celebration know this—that baptisms and weddings and funerals are times not just for alleluias, commitment to new life and communion, but also for expression of genuine grief and tears, letting go of the old life, and a sense of loss.

Yet these ministers of celebration know that the last word is resurrection. If people truly come with faith, their response to both pain and joy is that they want to praise the God of healing and hope. Our liturgies are dead often because our faith is dead, but they are also dead because we found there Groucho's ministers who took joy out of the world. We need leaders of celebration who truly believe in Easter.

Reminders and Dreamers

The extremes are antiquarians who lose the present with rites pulled from the dustbins of the fourth century, and space cadets who lose the past by reducing the Eucharist to hamburgers and coke.

We need reminders of our past, because we celebrate not just our own story but our people's stories. We "do this in memory" of those who have gone before us—primarily Jesus, who has revealed that our story need not be a dead end. We gather to celebrate precisely because we have come to believe that we are not alone, that we are part of a tradition, a heritage of people who give us hope because they have been on the same journey of dying and rising. Good ministers of celebration are people who remind us, who stir our memories to faith and hope, who expose us to signs and symbols with roots beyond our own limited times so that we recall we are a people in communion.

That people, however, is a community of hopes and dreams; people who believe that in Jesus' Resurrection the future has already begun. We celebrate with the Risen Lord who reaches out to us from our future, who is Real Presence with us now to give a taste of the yet to be. Good ministers of celebration are people who believe there is something new under the sun. They gather us in hope to strain toward the future. They expose us to signs and symbols which tell us that we are a pilgrim people who can never capture our God in any liturgical gesture or vesture because he always remains ahead of us, beckoning us into his future.

Listeners and Proclaimers

Talk of listeners brings to mind those "feminine" ministries—those so-called feminine traits of listening, receptivity, openness. Good ministers of celebration have ventured out of the sanctuary to listen to the stories of people. They read not only the rubrics but the signs of the times. They have lived with their fellow celebrants who are part and parcel of their own stories of faith. Their own stories took shape especially when they listened to Jesus.

Therefore, when they lead us in liturgy, their words and music and prayer and gesture proclaim not only their stories but our stories and God's story. We say, "Aha!" to their proclaiming. "Yes, that's what we have been going through. That's our dying and rising. That's the dying and rising of Jesus. You listened well; therefore, you speak well our faith, our hope, and our love."

A final word. Of course, at liturgy we are all celebrants. All of us are in some sense ministers of celebration. We all bring faith; and we all sing, reflect, pray, and gesture to express our joy. If we choose and ordain ministers to lead us in celebration, it is because we discern in them most clearly what we all should be: people who die and rise, remind and dream, listen and proclaim.

These are the qualities to look for in persons we install as Eucharistic ministers—those people who not only serve the bread and the cup at table in our churches but who also unite the community in church with the elderly, the sick, and the shut-ins by bringing the bread and wine to table in their homes. The care and reverence which these Eucharistic ministers show for the sick is one of the most inspiring signs of life in our Church today. They are able to spend time with people, far more than did the priest who was often rushing to some fifty homes on the first Friday of the month. Often, they also bring families with them to pray with those who cannot pray in church.

I know one pastor who "trains" these Eucharistic ministers only by showing them how to unlock the tabernacle. The training should be preparation to be Eucharistic men and women—celebrating ministers who have reason to celebrate because they have reflected upon their own stories of death and life. They have asked questions about the meaning of their stories. They have found that meaning only in communion with others, but no others fully satisfy their longing for healing and hope other than the One whom they name God. With that faith, they are prepared to be ministers of celebrating.

Conversation Starters

The format for the conversation starters is a little different for this chapter. The first question lists a number of possible events in your life, painful and joyful. Choose one of them (or add one of your own) and, in order, apply the following questions to that event. The process follows the steps suggested in this chapter which might lead you to move from human experience to religious experience, from your personal story to the celebration of God's presence in your story. After taking these steps with one event, on other occasions you can return and choose other events for the process.

1) When was the last time . . .

    someone close to you died?

    you entered a new, close friendship?

    you cried?

    a close friend left the priesthood or religious life?

    someone close to you got a divorce?

    someone forgave you?

    you forgave someone else?

    a baby was born in your family?

    you took a strong stand on an issue of justice?

    you felt trapped?

    someone close to you got married?

    you made an important change of vocation?

    you felt your age?

    you thought about death?

    you experienced the inspiring conversion of someone?

    you helped someone talk about his or her deepest hopes or fears?

you felt depressed?
you were captured by the beauty of nature?
you were seriously ill?
you experienced healing?
you experienced prejudice or injustice?
you felt guilty?
one of your children left home?
you felt respected and good about yourself?
you worried about the faith of your children?

2) List the feelings you had at the time of one of the above events.

3) What important questions did that event and those feelings raise?

4) Did those feelings and questions lead you into dependence on or union with others?
Name the others:

5) Did those feelings and questions lead you into dependence on or a relationship with God, with Jesus, with the Holy Spirit?

6) Did that relationship affect your prayer or show up in liturgical celebration?

7) Did you take any actions as a result of all of this?

Where I Stand

1) If I could relive one week of my life, I would choose . . .

2) The last time I thought seriously of suicide was . . .

3) Four critical turning points in my autobiography are . . .

4) My next important future decision will be about . . .

5) With the person I love most, I still can't seem to be completely united in the area of . . .

6) I believe in God the Father who . . .

7) I believe in Jesus who . . .

8) I believe in the Holy Spirit who . . .

9) The liturgical celebration which touched me most deeply was . . .

7 Ministries of Serving-Healing

Where I Stand

1) I was with a dying person when . . .

2) The most self-giving and selfless person I have known is . . .

3) My biggest failure has been . . .

4) I feel our welfare system for the poor is . . .

5) I most needed God when . . .

6) Three groups of alienated and rejected people today are . . .

7) When I hear the term "politician" I think of the following three words . . .

8) My experience of permanent deacons is . . . .

Elie Wiesel, in *Night*, tells of an execution that took place during his time at Buna, a Nazi concentration camp. Wiesel and the other prisoners were herded at gunpoint to assemble before three gallows. Two adults and a young boy were about to die as punishment for breaking camp rules—in order to educate the other prisoners in the folly of disobedience. The three stood on chairs with nooses round their necks. At a sign from the head of the camp, the three chairs were struck aside. Then the march past began, and each prisoner had to look death in the face. When Wiesel passed by, the two adults were no longer alive. But the third rope was still moving; since he was so light, the child was still alive. Wiesel writes:

For more than half an hour he stayed there, struggling between life and death, dying in slow agony under our eyes. And we had to look him full in the face. He was still alive when I passed in front of him. His tongue was still red, his eyes not yet glazed.

Behind me, I heard a man asking: "Where is God now?" And I heard a voice within me answer him: "Where is he? Here he is—he is hanging here on this gallows. . . ."

In one sense, all ministries are service. When theologians single out ministries of service as a special dimension of the Christian mission, they speak especially of those ministries which image the God who empties himself to hang on the gallows with us.

Kenosis

The biblical word for that is *kenosis*: the emptying forth, the self-giving love, the pouring out of God's life that his people might live. The God of some Eastern religions is remote—unapproachable and unapproaching. The God of Greek philosophy, which influenced some Christian theology, is steady as a rock, unchangeable, a Prime Mover who can't be moved. The God of the Bible hangs on the Cross with us. He is a God of passion who feels our pain and our joy, who reaches out to us in our most empty and abandoned times when we feel most powerless. He does not snatch us out of those times or take us down from the Cross but hangs there with us and reveals the real power in self-giving love.

That love climaxes in Jesus, and St. Paul marvels at that in the great New Testament passage on *kenosis*:

His state was divine, yet he did not cling to his equality with God but *emptied himself* to assume the condition of a slave, and became as men are; and being as all men are, he was humbler yet, even to accepting death, death on a cross. [Phil. 2:6-8]

The Jesus who is himself humble and humbled, whose life is emptied out in tears and blood, and who hangs on a cross has come especially for those who also are humble and powerless, who know tears and who shed blood, and who hang on their own unique cross.

The monks of Qumran, the Jewish desert community at about the time of Jesus, had the following rule:

> No madman, or lunatic, or simpleton, or fool, no blind man, or maimed, or lame, or deaf man, and no minor, shall enter into the Community, for the Angels of Holiness are with them.

Yet, when the disciples of John ask Jesus if he is "He who is to come," Jesus tells them to look to those he welcomes into his community and to check out the words of Isaiah, who knew better than Qumran the people with whom the Messiah would spend his time:

> Go back and report to John what you hear and see: the blind recover their sight, cripples walk, lepers are cured, the deaf hear, dead men are raised to life, and the poor have the good news preached to them. [Matt. 11:4-6]

Jesus knew that the poor might hear the Good News about the gift of God's mercy and love. Unlike some Jews who really believed that they were self-made men who earned salvation by following the Law and by their own power, the powerless were more ready to believe that healing, mercy, reconciliation, and salvation were not their own products but gifts of a merciful God. Jesus lived a life like theirs and reveals that it is precisely in human powerlessness and death that the gift of resurrection occurs. Therefore, Paul can proclaim the absolute foolishness of God which baffles Jews and Gentiles who look for salvation not through weakness but through power.

> While the Jews demand miracles and the Greeks look for wisdom, here are we preaching a crucified Christ; to the Jews an obstacle that they cannot get over; to the pagans madness, but to those who have been called, whether they are Jews or Greeks, a Christ who is the power and the wisdom of God. For God's foolishness is wiser than human wisdom, and God's weakness is stronger than human strength. [1 Cor. 1:22-25]

The gospel of that same Christ calls us to that foolishness and that weakness. In Michael Buckley's letter to Jesuit ordinands, his comments on the weakness of priests applies to all ministers of serving-healing. He says we make a fatal error if we transfer the corporation executive's criteria for leadership to priesthood and ministry in the Church. Business looks at gifts, talents, skills, and matches gifts with careers. The key question is—what are his or her gifts? Certainly, to avoid some kind of masochism or sadism we need to raise that question for ministries. But there is also a different question. Is that man weak enough to be a priest; is this woman fragile enough to be a servant-healer? Is this person vulnerable enough so that he/she cannot banish suffering from life, so that she feels what it is to be an ordinary woman who shares the human journey and stumbles and bumbles along the path we all share? Does he know fear, loneliness, failure, and self-doubt just as we all do, and still gather to offer Eucharist, to give thanks to the God who fills us precisely where we are empty? We ask these questions because we are really asking—is this person like Jesus the Christ, that profoundly weak man who reveals Good News to the poor and the powerless who still hang on the Cross?

Matthew tells us we shall be judged as Church on whether or not we share that same Good News with the poor. The criteria for judgment are what we have done to the hungry, the thirsty, the stranger, the naked, the sick, and the prisoner (cf. Matt. 25). That is the Good News. That is the gospel addressed to servant-healers who claim to be followers of the Crucified One. That is the gospel too often mutilated by the self-righteous who complain of welfare loafers (but not about subsidies to corporation loafers) and the shiftless poor who don't work (not a word about the shiftless rich who don't have to work).

Those who accept the gospel and reach out, like Jesus, especially to those most wounded, most alienated, most poor and powerless—those people enter the ministries of *diakonia*, of serving-healing, in our times. We might also call these ministries of reconciliation, ministeries of outreach to those most in need.

A key question, of course, is—who are the poor? Who are most in need? When Luke says in his version of the beatitudes, "Blessed are the poor," he is speaking of physical poverty. Matthew's version broadens our vision to include "the poor in spirit"; and someone has defined poverty of spirit as "Blessed are those who know they need God." We cannot limit needs to just the physical: poverty, hunger, thirst, etc. Many people in the middle class know they need God. Many people in upper middle class families know empty marriages and boring lives. But, as someone has said, at least the rich can afford marriage counselors and a summer vacation. Those who experience poverty of both body and spirit always have a special place in Christian ministries of serving-healing. We cannot close our eyes to devastated lives at home and abroad and then limit our concern to a chosen few in our own homes and neighborhoods simply because we realize that everyone hurts a little bit.

In the past, those who opened their eyes to human need offered their ministries of service in countless ways. Among those ministries we might include: ministry in hospitals, orphanages, homes for the aged; in the St. Vincent de Paul Society, the Legion of Mary, the Catholic Worker movement; the many ministries offered through Catholic Charities, social justice departments and committees; ministries to the handicapped, minority groups, farm workers, and other working people; ministry in the foreign and home missions; ministries through the Campaign for Human Development—as well as the many unorganized ways in which individual Christians imaged the God of love who hangs on the Cross with his people.

I hear people say today that among those people who feel most alienated and neglected we might include: Catholics who have divorced and remarried, divorced people who now live as single adults, young adults between the ages of eighteen and thirty, people with a homosexual orientation, elderly people, persons in prison. Perhaps a look at just a few ministries of service may help unveil further possibilities.

The Poor

Lest we be guilty of ministerial imperialism and restrict ministry to those who serve the poor, let us first proclaim that the poor also minister to and serve one another and the rest of the Church. Martin Luther King often used the parable of the Good Samaritan to insist that it is often the despised Samaritans, the powerless and disdained outcasts of the community, who reach down to bind up the wounds of prejudice, selfishness, and bigotry which afflict the so-called élite of the community. It is the poor who most often know they need God. It is regrettable that we turn more often to God out of our emptiness rather than in thanksgiving when our lives are full; but those people who become believers even in the midst of their pain can challenge people who live the "good life" to give thanks for their blessings and share those blessings with others.

A powerful instance of the strong being served and healed by the weak, the "big ones" by the "little ones" (the *anawim* of the Scriptures) is what happens at the Faith and Sharing Retreats initiated by Jean Vanier. The retreat gathers the "little ones"—the handicapped, the prisoner, the elderly, the poor—with the "big ones"—the rest of us who are supposedly healthy and whole. "We" often come to serve "them," and God throws a curve at us. It is "we" who are healed by "them." In one instance, during a retreat of some five hundred people, a bishop (taught to hide his feelings as a male and even more so as a bishop) found that a so-called mentally handicapped man named Roger simply insisted on hugging him and bulldogging him with affection. Who do you think was healed? Who was the minister?

The "little ones" also include those who have made themselves poor and powerless. Their witness serves not only the poor but the entire Church. Perhaps a few words from some of them might deepen our sense of service.

Mother Teresa of Calcutta, dedicated to the poorest of the poor and the hopelessly ill, declares: "The biggest disease today is not leprosy, but rather the feeling of being unwanted, uncared for, and deserted by everybody. The greatest evil is the lack of love, the terrible indifference toward one's neighbour who lives at the roadside assulted by exploitation, corruption, poverty, and disease."

Simone Weil, who died early through malnutrition because, as a friend said, she only felt at ease on the lowest rung of the social ladder, lost among the masses of poor and outcasts, says: "The love of neighbour in all its fullness simply means being able to say to him: 'What are you going through?' It is a recognition that the sufferer exists, not only as a unit in a collection or a specimen from the social category labeled 'unfortunate,' but as a man exactly like us who was one day stamped with a special mark of affliction."

Charles de Foucauld, who gave up his wealth to live in the African desert, offered an image of Jesus' poverty, simplicity, and care for those whom he called "the sickest souls, the most abandoned sheep": "Jesus came to Nazareth, the place of the hidden life, of ordinary family life: a life of prayer, work and obscurity, the silent virtues. . . . It was a humble, holy, obscure life of well-doing—the life of most human beings."

Most of us will not go to African deserts, but we all have our own Nazareths, and we all can live the hidden, silent, obscure life of Jesus offered in ministries of service.

Politicians

For so many people the word "politician" has become a dirty word. For many, politicians seem about as far removed as possible from the poor and powerless whom we have just heard. Yet, at least in one respect, the poor will remain powerless unless we have people who enter politics with a keen sense of service. It is not just private sin and injustice which keep people poor. It is sin and injustice built into the social system. It is the task of politicians to build more just systems.

Theologians today speak of "social sin." They refer to structures within a political, economic, or educational system that in themselves oppress human beings, stifle freedom, and impose gross injustice. They refer also to the involvement in these structures of persons who do not take responsibility for the evil done—e.g., a taxing structure which systematically, through loopholes and benefits, frees large corporations from paying equitable taxes and socks it to the middle class. The Roman Synod of bishops states in their *Justice in the World*:

> The faithful, particularly the more wealthy and comfortable among them, simply do not see structural social injustice as a sin, simply feel no personal responsibility for it and simply feel no obligation to do anything about it. . . . To live like Dives with Lazarus at the gate is not even perceived as sinful. [no. 7]

In times when the world economic system finds both oil-producing countries and food-producing countries raising prices which make the poorest nations even poorer, in times when the United States' welfare structures systematically encourage the breakup of families and discourage work, in times when some states tax the sale of food, drugs, and other goods which are necessities for the poor and the elderly, we need not only Mother Teresas who heal the wounds of individuals. We also need politicians who attack the injustice built into the system. We need politicians skilled in what politics has to be, the "art of the possible," politicians who know how to get legislation through; but we also need politicians skilled in the values of the gospel to offer their lives through ministries of service to those most mangled by the system.

Deacons

Finally, we come to ministers who receive their very name from the ministry of *diakonia*.

I do not intend to enter the controversy concerning whether or not we should have in the Church the restored permanent diaconate. The controversy centers largely around the issue of clericalism: has the Church created a new brand of clerics whose status comes from role rather than personal gift and weakness and who create, once again, the impression that ministry is reserved for those who receive official recognition and ordination? Does this new breed of "professionals" discourage "non-professional" servant-healers?

I know deacons who are truly men of the world, in fact, somewhat anti-clerical; who are present to the weak out of their own weakness rather than their power as clerics. I also know deacons who are super-clerics, who love to dress up in clerical regalia. I know pastoral theologians who hold that the permanent diaconate is a stepping-stone to a married priesthood and to the ordination of women. I also know of African bishops, among the first to ordain deacons, who have stopped ordaining because they felt deacons denigrated the ministries of other lay people. I know of one director of a diaconate program who says, "Some men need the diaconate more than the diaconate needs them."

The very meaning of *diakonia* and the spirituality of servant-healer, weak and poor as the crucified Jesus, should lop off any budding heads of clericalism, power-plays, and the drive for role and status. Although there is a controversy about whether we should have deacons, in fact we have them. A greater concern should be with what deacons do, or better, with what deacons should be. They should be "diaconal men."

Just as priests *do* many things, and have many functions, I have already suggested that central to the *being* of priests is that they are mystagogues—men who have tasted the mysteries of death and life and who can initiate others into the mysteries, Eucharistic men. Deacons also *do* many things. The question is—out of what spirituality do they come? What kind of men *are* they? The spirituality of serving-healing, the ministry of imaging Jesus who hangs on the Cross with his people, the union with the foolish, powerless, weak, and poor Son of Man who has no place to put his head offers an identity and *way of being* to all to enter the diaconal ministry of servant-healer.

It might also touch what deacons do. At present, some deacons do ministries which seem more appropriate for catechists, liturgists, or others. If the heart of the ministry of servant-healer is offering the presence of the self-giving Jesus through images of union with the poor and the weak, it seems that the actions of deacons should touch especially the most poor, the most alienated, rejected, and unloved.

I shall conclude by returning to a Nazi concentration camp, this time to one described by Viktor Frankl in his book, *Man's Search for Meaning*. His comrades came to him asking why they should not commit suicide.

> I told my comrades that human life, under any circumstances, never ceases to have a meaning, and that this infinite meaning of life includes suffering and dying, privation and death. I asked the poor creatures who listened to me attentively in the darkness of the hut to face up to the seriousness of our position. They must not lose hope but should keep their courage in the certainty that the hopelessness of our struggle did not detract from its dignity and its meaning. I said that someone looks down on each of us in difficult hours—a friend, a wife, somebody alive or dead, or a God—and he would not expect us to disappoint him. He would hope to find us suffering proudly—not miserably—knowing how to die.

Christian ministers of serving and healing serve a God who not only looks on us and expects us to know how to die. We serve a God who has become one of us and knows how to die, who hangs with us on the Cross.

Conversation Starters

1) How would you feel about watching an execution?

2) Do you believe God feels our pain?

3) Does any group you belong to exclude any persons?

4) Have you ever been physically poor?

5) Would you like your priests to be free of self-doubt and failure?

6) Do you know divorced and remarried people who would like to be reconciled with the Church?

7) What is your parish doing with the eighteen-to-thirty-year-olds?

8) What is your parish doing with the elderly?

9) Have you ever been surprised when a "little one" ministered to you?

10) Can you identify three "social sins" in unjust systems in your community?

11) Do you support affirmative action programs in hiring minorities to correct injustices of the past?

12) Do you believe the Church should ordain permanent deacons?

Where I Stand

1) I was with a dying person when . . .

2) The most self-giving and selfless person I have known is . . .

3) My biggest failure has been . . .

4) I feel our welfare system for the poor is . . .

5) I most needed God when . . .

6) Three groups of alienated and rejected people today are . . .

7) When I hear the term "politician" I think of the following three words . . .

8) My experience of permanent deacons is . . . .

8 From Ministries to Institutions to Ministries . . .

Where I Stand

1) When the term "minister" is applied to me, I feel . . .

2) I feel ministries are made trivial if . . .

3) I feel ministries are clericalized when . . .

4) Of the four dimensions of ministry, my strongest is . . .

5) My weakest of the four dimensions is . . .

6) Our parish spends most of its time, energy, and money on the ministry of . . .

7) Our parish spends the least of its time, energy, and money on the ministry of . . .

8) My most important ministry in the world is . . .

9) I believe Christian ministry is . . .

There is some concern today about an indiscriminate use of the word "ministry," a use contrary to custom. For that reason, I was tempted to raise the issue in the very first chapter. I hope the preceding chapters give us, at this point, a better context in which to raise the issues.

One concern is that some use "ministry" so broadly that it eventually means nothing and becomes trivial. We are a bit startled when we hear someone proclaim, "Baking muffins for the church bazaar is my ministry"; or "Bartending is my ministry." (We must admit, however, that the author of the popular song, "Set 'Em Up, Joe," may be looking to his local bartender for serving and healing.)

Another concern, expressed in the late seventies by a group of long-time Chicago leaders in the lay apostolate, is that much talk of ministry has been limited exclusively to church-related actions. Historically ministry does refer to ministries in the Church. But to declare that all lay people by their baptism are called to ministry in the Church may seem, to some ears, to exclude lay people's primary call, which is to service in the world.

In view of these concerns, the bishops of West Germany note in their declaration on ministry that the service of lay people to the world does not constitute a ministry in the theological sense. Rev. James Coriden suggests that we should distinguish between ministry, which is a position of leadership in the Church—officially recognized in some way by the institutional Church—and Christian witness, to which all believers are called by baptism. This leads, however, to a further concern: over the centuries the clericalization of ministries, at least in the Roman Catholic tradition, has limited the term to ordained clerics.

In view of all these issues, might it be better to expand the limits of the term "ministry," especially during this time after Vatican II when we are struggling to act upon wider images of Church as community and not just institution? Does the narrow, institutionalized definition of ministry perhaps stifle the Spirit who seems to be spreading gifts laterally with little attention to institutional forms? "Serving in a Ministerial Church," published by the National Federation of Priests' Councils (note: a group of clerics!), attempts to listen to this freedom of the Spirit. It declares: "Ministry is the activity of the Church as it is carried out by all members, at every level and under the inspiration of the Spirit."

Richard McBrien attempts to thread his way through the maze by speaking of ministry in the strict sense and in the broad sense:

> A ministry, in the strict theological sense, must be officially designated by the Church as a ministry.
>
> That doesn't mean that the pope or some Vatican congregation must explicitly approve. It means only that some specific Christian community recognizes it has a need, and then proceeds to select individuals who might be qualified to meet the need. . . . Ministry also has a wider, less tech-

nical meaning. It is a term which can apply to any act of Christian service. Ministry, in this broader sense, is making Christ, the Suffering Servant of God, present to the world, and especially to those in need. [Richard P. McBrien, "The New Call to Ministry," *St. Anthony's Messenger*, March, 1979, p. 22.]

Top-Down or Bottom-Up Ministries

It should be clear that this book has adopted McBrien's broader use of the term "ministry." My concern, however, has gone beyond the niceties of precise theological language. My concern has been with our very image of God, Christ, and Church.

John Shea states that an image of Church as *institution*, with structures of belief, ritual, laws, and official ministries, will generally take a "top-down" approach which stresses the transcendence of God and his separation from human life, the divinity of Christ as his heavenly messenger, and a hierarchical Church of pope, bishops, and clergy who give the message *to the people*. This will separate the rulers from the ruled, the ministers from those ministered to—or, to use Johnny Carson's terms, the "givers from the givees." The danger is that, since pope and bishops and clerics are seen closest to God, they can begin to dictate downward the style of his Church and become isolated from the people. Then ministry may very easily be carried out on the terms of the clerics and not on the actual needs of the rest of the Church. We would be hard pressed to deny that most of us grew up in the top-down Church.

But when the Church is turned upside down (or, better, downside up), when God is seen as imaged and imminent in all his people, imaged in Jesus who is one with humankind, and imaged forever in all those touched by the Spirit of the Risen Christ, then we have a "bottom-up Church" in which ministries arise out of all the gifts spread out in all the people. Ministries become ministries *of the people*. Although not all will respond to the gifts of God, this situates ministries within the total giftedness of the community. We are back to a *community* image of Church in which ministries become not the private preserve of the few but the possible vocation of all. (John Shea, "Notes Toward a Theology of Ministry," *Chicago Studies,* Fall, 1978, pp. 325-326.)

Gerard Egan describes this as a shift from a few designated ministers to a ministering congregation, and from vertical ministry, where the few deliver one-to-one services, to lateral ministry where the designated ministers support and challenge the entire community to minister to each other ("The Parish: Ministering Community and Community of Ministers," in *The Parish in Community and Ministry,* ed. by Evelyn Eaton Whitehead. New York: Paulist Press, 1978, pp. 73-90). It is a shift from what we described in chapter five as *institution* distributing services to *community* in which members serve each other.

In this book, I have taken the position that this time in history may be much like those exciting New Testament times regarding emerging ministries. This has resulted in a broad use of the term "ministry." After many centuries of clericalization (although people went on ministering without Church permission or approval), we are now experiencing a new Pentecost launching people into the streets to share the Spirit's gifts. Ministries originally emerged out of the ebullient Pauline faith in the universality of the presence of Christ's Spirit: "There is a variety of gifts but always the same Spirit; there are all sorts of service to be done, but always the same Lord; working in all sorts of different ways in different people, it is the same God who is working in all of them" (1 Cor. 12:4-6). Talk about a "bottom-up Church"!

The process was hardly neat and tidy in Corinth. It will not be any more tidy today. In the process, some will claim the term "ministry" without precise theological sophistication. That is what I find in talking with people. People who just a few years ago scoffed at ministry as a term limited to Protestants are now claiming it as their own. At least some people like the term, and I have found that they resist the strict use by some theologians. It seems a bit arrogant to take the term away from them. The key issue is not the term but the image of God, Christ, and Church which is coming into being. I suggest we can, therefore, endure some birthpains as we struggle to find ways to talk about this new vision of Church and the new sense of responsibility which springs from our vision. I also suggest we can avoid trivializing the term by defining ministry through the *quality* of what is done (in Word, community-building, celebrating, and serving-healing), whether or not there is official institutional recognition.

I believe that our times offer some of the excitement of those early centuries which were marked by great flexibility and adaptation to people's needs when Christians sought ways to put their gifts in touch with those needs. Perhaps a brief foray into those times would encourage that same creativity and flexibility in us. Jaroslav Pelikan, the great Church historian, quotes the Russian writer, Berdyaev, in asserting that *traditions* are the dead faith of living people, and *Tradition* is the living faith of dead people. A look into history may free us from rigid traditions about ministries (and perhaps also about language concerning ministries) and release us for the living faith of Tradition which seeks ever new ways to share and express the Good News.

A Look into History

In the early Church one of those ways to share and express the Good News was the ministry of presbyter—but the functions of those presbyters were very different from those of contemporary priests. The 1941 ritual, with which many of today's priests were ordained, spoke of priesthood in terms of two powers—the power to offer sacrifice for the living and the dead, and the power to forgive sins. In the third century, these powers belonged only to the bishops. The crucial sentence regarding presbyters in the third century Ritual of Hypolytus read, "O God and Father of Our Lord Jesus Christ, look upon this thy servant and impart to him the spirit of grace and the gift of the presbyterate that he may be able to direct thy people with a pure heart." That's all.

Historian Gregory Dix states that the primitive Christian presbytery, like the Jewish from which it was developed, was a corporate, judicial, and administrative body with the bishop as its president. The presbyters at first had no liturgical function; the bishop was the great liturgist. By the fourth century, however, bishop and presbyter passed each other going in opposite directions. Due to the spread of Christianity and the increase of churches, the bishop became the administrator of a large territory and the presbyters became the liturgists for the local community.

Development, adapting to people's needs, flexibility—these are the qualities which mark the emergence of ministries in the early Church. Scripture scholar Eugene Maly writes in *The Priest and Sacred Scripture*, "We should not expect to find a clearly formulated definition of Christian ministry from the beginning, or at any single point in the development of New Testament revelation. Christian ministry was never 'frozen' in any one mold but continued to develop and to be adapted in the succeeding moments of history. Such development and adaptation continued even in the post-biblical age. . . .

Development itself is canonical and therefore normative." The United States bishops' document, *Ministries in the Church: Study Text Three,* states: "It is doubtful that a single ecclesiastical office remains today in the same form as the New Testament Churches employed it."

That does not mean everything is up for grabs. I have suggested that ministries of Word, community-building, celebrating, and serving-healing are dimensions of biblical faith and that the faith of believers today will find new ways to personify that faith. But these ministries come first; then come the offices, institutions, and traditions which Christians find to express those ministries. This places the criteria for genuine ministry in the *quality* of what is being done and in the *faith* of the person doing it, rather than just in official recognition. If the person or community in its faith-commitment to the Lord is searching for ways to image God in Word, community-building, celebrating, and serving-healing, then it is enfleshing in ministries the Tradition of living faith of the people of God.

This broad view of ministry, then, means that all Christians are called to incarnate in their own way those four dimensions of ministry. Without using the word "ministry," Christians have done this for centuries. If this extended meaning of the term helps us view the entire Church as a ministerial people, if it helps de-clericalize ministry so that the gifts of the Spirit might be more widely shared, if it does not become trivial and just one more piece of jargon, then the Church will become more effectively a "we" rather than a "they"—those official ministers "over there" before whom "we" are merely passive receivers.

Recognition of Ministries

With that in mind, if we do choose to commission, install, ordain, and officially recognize people as ministers, we need to keep several things in mind. First, such official recognition does not create ministry. The document on ministry by the National Federation of Priests' Councils states: "It is not that ministries exist because they are recognized by ordained ministers. It is because ministries exist that they should be recognized." Persons should be ordained priests or deacons because they are already ministering as priests and deacons. By ordination, the community should be saying to that person, "We rejoice in your gifts. You have been serving us well. We want to officially recognize your service so that you know we support you and to allow you more effectively to witness to what we all should be."

That brings up a second point. Official recognition through commissioning, installing, or ordaining should never relieve a community from the responsibilities of ministering but rather challenge others to live the gospel as effectively as the one being recognized. One American bishop has refused to ordain deacons until his diocese has training programs and installation rituals for other ministries which will be officially recognized by the diocese—an attempt to help people see that not only clerics are ministers. There may be good reason to compare our times with New Testament times. In those times, the fullness of time, Jesus as a layman shook up the institutions of the Jewish community and released the Spirit into all sorts of new gifts and ministries. After centuries of institutions which have become so clerical, perhaps we need to shake them up, let the ministeries emerge in an atmosphere of freedom and not try to control them too quickly by official recognition. That might encourage more people to see themselves as ministers.

Finally, if we do recognize ministries especially for service in the Church, we need to remember that most Christians will minister *in the world* without official recognition. In *Religious Pilgrimage*, Jean Haldane writes:

> Behaviorally the institution's message is to equate church organization work with "real" lay ministry—and the rewards are for those who do this. . . . It ought to be possible to validate membership in the church and *ministry in the secular sector* as being bona fide lay ministry—an outreach of the church. . . . We do not have to manufacture programs of lay ministry—it is *already happening* as lay people interact with the world day by day.

In this book, our discussions of ministers as story-tellers, prophets, educators, poets, lovers, parents, the poor, politicians, reminders and dreamers, listeners and proclaimers were attempts to move ministry beyond the church sanctuary—a step which might even move us to listen to our friendly neighborhood bartender!

I shall close with some imagery from Henri Nouwen. Nouwen says that each of us is like a huge rock, with walls and barriers that keep others out and keep us secure. But, year by year, God keeps carving away at that rock. We thought we knew what our marriage would be and something said, "No!" to that. We thought we knew what priesthood would be and something said, "No!" to that. We thought we knew what ministry was and something said, "No!" to that. We feel tired and frustrated, powerless, unable to change ourselves or others.

Then we discover one day that God's hand has created some empty space in that rock. We discover a cave hewn out of the stone. We find we have space to welcome people, people who also are so weary, so tired, so in need of a place to gather where they will not feel alone. They come in and say to us, "Oh, I see you too are a rock dweller. You have some empty space into which I might enter. You know what I have been going through, and you won't force your plans on me, manipulate me, or try to control me. You offer a place where I can be me."

God's carving hand seems especially at work in our days, both on us as individuals and on the entire Church. Once again, God is creating some empty space. We feel the pain of loss, because part of that emptiness is a loss of traditions—traditions about ministry which have been with us for centuries. There is also the joy of discovery, though, because in our emptiness we are forced back to Tradition—not just the forms and institutions but the living faith out of which ministries will emerge. That empty space leaves room for God to carve us more fully into his image. There is also room for God's people to come in and hear some Good News, experience new bonds of communion, rejoice, and celebrate because finally they have found someone who has room for them, and they feel the gentle touch of one who serves and heals. This is Christian ministry: allowing God to be present in us to form us in his image, and then welcoming his people into some sacred space where we can share the gifts of our God.

Conversation Starters

1) Do you believe the approach to ministries in this book has been too broad or too narrow?

2) Is your approach to God, Jesus, Church and ministries "top-down" or "bottom-up"?

3) Which of the four dimensions of ministry is strongest in your bishop?

4) Which is strongest in your priest?

5) Do you agree that what we do (in terms of Word, community-building, and celebrating, and serving-healing) should have some bearing on what is called Christian ministry?

6) Do you agree that a person should act as described above with conscious faith in order to be a Christian minister?

7) Do you believe most priests and deacons minister as such before they are ordained?

8) Do you believe ordination of priests and their presence in a parish stimulates or decreases the active involvement of others in church ministries?

9) When did you last minister in the world?

10) When did God say his loudest "No!" to your plans and designs for your life?

11) Who was the last person you let enter deeply into your life?

Where I Stand

1) When the term "minister" is applied to me, I feel . . .

2) I feel ministries are made trivial if . . .

3) I feel ministries are clericalized when . . .

4) Of the four dimensions of ministry, my strongest is . . .

5) My weakest of the four dimensions is . . .

6) Our parish spends most of its time, energy, and money on the ministry of . . .

7) Our parish spends the least of its time, energy, and money on the ministry of . . .

8) My most important ministry in the world is . . .

9) I believe Christian ministry is . . .

Select Bibliography

The following references include some of the seminal theoretical resources which ground the more popular approach of this book. There are also references to some recent publications on ministries which extend and apply some of the important themes of this book.

Barbour, Ian G. *Myths, Models and Paradigms*. New York: Harper and Row, 1974.

Berger, Peter L. *A Rumor of Angels*. Garden City, NY: Doubleday, 1970.

———. *The Sacred Canopy: Elements of a Sociological Theory of Religion*. Garden City, NY: Doubleday, 1969.

Berryman, Jerome, ed. *Life Maps: Conversations on the Journey of Faith with Jim Fowler and Sam Keen*. Waco, TX: Word Books, 1978.

Brown, Raymond E. *Priest and Bishop: Biblical Reflections*. New York: Paulist Press, 1970.

Capon, Robert Farrar. *Hunting the Divine Fox: Images and Mystery in the Christian Faith*. New York: The Seabury Press, 1974.

Cooke, Bernard. *Ministry to Word and Sacraments: History and Theology*. Philadelphia: Fortress Press, 1976.

Downs, Thomas. *A Journey to Self Through Dialogue: An Excursion of Spiritual Self-discovery for Individuals and Groups*. West Mystic, CT: Twenty-third Publications, 1977.

———. *The Parish as Learning Community*. New York: Paulist Press, 1979.

Dulles, Avery. *Models of the Church: A Critical Assessment of the Church in All Its Aspects*. Garden City, NY: Doubleday, 1974.

Dunning, James B. "The Rite of Christian Initiation of Adults: Model of Adult Growth." *Worship* 53 (1979): 142-156.

Durka, Gloria, and Smith, Joanmarie, eds. *Aesthetic Dimensions of Religious Education*. New York: Paulist Press, 1979.

Eigo, Francis A., ed. *Ministering in a Servant Church*. Villanova, PA: Villanova University Press, 1978.

Geaney, Dennis. *Emerging Lay Ministries*. Kansas City: Andrews and McMeel, 1979.

Gilkey, Langdon. *Naming the Whirlwind: The Renewal of God-Language*. New York: Bobbs-Merrill, 1969.

Girzaitis, Loretta. *The Church as Reflecting Community: Models of Adult Religious Learning*. West Mystic, CT: Twenty-third Publications, 1977.

Greeley, Andrew M. *The Great Mysteries: An Essential Catechism.* New York: Seabury Press, 1976.

_____ . *Unsecular Man: The Persistence of Religion.* New York: Schocken Books, 1972.

Haldane, Jean M. *Religious Pilgrimage.* Washington, D.C.: Alban Institute, 1975.

Hater, Robert J. *The Ministry Explosion: A New Awareness of Every Christian's Call to Minister.* Dubuque, IA: Wm. C, Brown, 1979.

Holmes, Urban T., III. *Ministry and Imagination.* New York: Seabury Press, 1976.

_____ . *The Priest in Community: Exploring the Roots of Ministry.* New York: Seabury Press, 1978.

Keating, Charles J. *Community: Learning to Live in Diocesan, Religious, and Parish Communities.* West Mystic, CT: Twenty-third Publications, 1977.

Lonergan, Bernard. *Method in Theology.* London: Darton, Longman & Todd, 1972.

Lynch, William. *Christ and Prometheus: A New Image of the Secular.* Notre Dame, IN: University of Notre Dame Press, 1970.

Maly, Eugene H. *The Priest and Sacred Scripture.* Washington, D.C.: USCC Publications, 1972.

Maslow, Abraham. *Religions, Values, and Peak-Experiences.* New York: The Viking Press, 1970.

Mayerhoff, Milton. *On Caring.* New York: Harper and Row, 1971.

Mead, Loren B. *Lay Ministry: A Tool Kit.* Washington, D.C.: The Alban Institute, 1976.

Nouwen, Henri. *Creative Ministry.* Garden City, NY: Doubleday, 1971.

_____ . *The Wounded Healer: Ministry in Contemporary Society.* Garden City, NY: Doubleday, 1972.

Novak, Michael. *Ascent of the Mountain, Flight of the Dove.* New York: Harper and Row, 1971.

Rahner, Karl. "Christology within an Evolutionary View of the World." *Theological Investigations, Vol. V.* Baltimore: Helicon Press, 1966.

_____ . "The Concept of Mystery in Catholic Theology," and "On the Theology of the Incarnation," and "Nature and Grace," and "The Theology of Symbol." *Theological Investigations, Vol. IV.* Baltimore: Helicon Press, 1966.

_____ . *Hominization: The Evolutionary Origin of Man as a Theological Problem.* New York: Herder and Herder, 1965.

Saint Anthony Messenger. "Special Issue: Lay Ministry." March, 1979.

Shea, John. "Notes Toward a Theology of Ministry." *Chicago Studies* 17 (1978): 317-330.

_____ . *Stories of God: An Unauthorized Biography.* Chicago: The Thomas More Press, 1978.

Shepherd, William C. *Man's Condition: God and the World Process.* New York: Herder and Herder, 1969.

Simons, George F. *Keeping Your Personal Journal.* New York: Paulist Press, 1978.

Smith, John E. *Experience and God.* New York: Oxford University Press, 1968.

Storr, Anthony. *The Dynamics of Creation.* New York: Atheneum, 1972.

United States Bishops' Committee on the Liturgy. *Study Text III: Ministries in the Church.* Washington, D.C.: USCC Publications, 1974.

Whitehead, Evelyn Eaton, ed. *The Parish in Community and Ministry.* New York: Paulist Press, 1978.